THE SPACE BETWEEN STRATEGY AND EXECUTION

8 Pillars to Successful Business Transformation

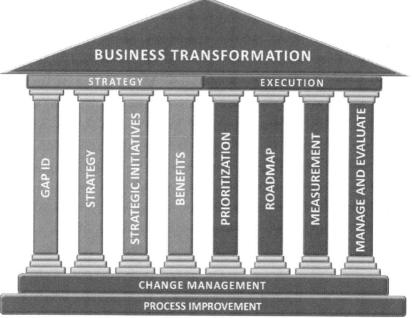

The Harden Transformation Framework ©

Disclaimer: This book contains advice and information. The publisher and author disclaim liability for any psychological or medical outcomes that may occur as a result of any of the suggestions in this book.

Published by Gregg Harden.

ISBN: 978-1-7336464-2-0

For more information contact:

Gregg Harden: greggharden@gmail.com

Legal Disclaimer:

The author and publisher of this book and the accompanying materials have used their best efforts in preparing this book. The information contained in this book is strictly for educational purposes. Therefore, if you wish to apply ideas contained in this book, you are taking full responsibility for your actions.

Your level of success in attaining the results claimed in our materials depends on the time you devote to the program, ideas and techniques mentioned, your finances, knowledge and various skills. Since these factors differ according to individuals, we cannot guarantee your success. Nor are we responsible for any of your actions. Many factors will be important in determining your actual results and no guarantees are made that you will achieve results similar to ours or anybody else's. In fact, no guarantees are made that you will achieve any results from our ideas and techniques in our material.

The author and publisher disclaim any warranties (express or implied), merchantability, or fitness for any particular purpose. The author and publisher shall in no event be held liable to any party for any direct, indirect, punitive, special, incidental or other consequential damages arising directly or indirectly from any use of this material, which is provided "as is", and without warranties.

The author and publisher do not warrant the performance, effectiveness or applicability of any sites listed or linked to in this report. All links are for informational purposes only and are not warranted for content, accuracy or any other implied or explicit purpose.

TABLE OF CONTENTS

INTRODUCTION

THE SPACE BETWEEN

BILLION-DOLLAR EXECUTION

People love to talk about a "billion-dollar idea". Not just fresh graduates and young executives, but even senior management and seasoned entrepreneurs are fascinated by this notion. Of course, the most successful of them are equally concerned, if not more, about execution.

"Execution is the game."

- Gary Vaynerchuck

After twenty-five years of business consulting, I have no doubts about the power of execution. Without execution, an idea is nothing. A strategy is nothing. I have seen many companies focus on strategy while minimizing the importance of planning and execution. These companies have paid the price for their reluctance to embrace the power of a plan and the criticality of execution. Just because you wrote it down doesn't mean it will actually happen. Companies must focus more on the space between strategy and execution.

Aptly titled "The Space Between," this book provides a clear perspective of how to cover the space between a business strategy and its desired outcomes.

"Strategy execution is the responsibility that makes or breaks executives."

- Alan Branche

Execution can mean different things: new technology, new operations, or a new focus. Often, it is a combination of several elements. Good execution is about translating "strategic intent" into "everyday actions." It is about putting your business culture to work. It is about committing to an identity instead of simply focusing on blatant growth. It is about a million other things that vary from business to business.

But all these can be positioned into a fairly universal model. To demystify the process, I have distilled the best practices of superior execution into eight well-defined phases. These are:

1. Gap Identification
2. Strategy
3. Strategic Initiatives
4. Benefits
5. Prioritization
6. Roadmap
7. Metrics Measurement
8. Manage & Evaluate

Through these eight stages, an organization can transform itself and achieve its desired results. Successful business transformation can mean the difference between a company reaching new heights of success or closing down.

The business transformation process is similar regardless of industry or solution. The same principles apply to:

- New software that needs to be implemented

- New business processes that need to be developed

- New resources that need to be added

- New products that need to be identified and launched

- New marketing plans that should expand brand awareness through social media interaction or through typical marketing and branding tactics.

All these things are in some way an effort to transform a business. And the principles of identifying where we have a gap, what we need to be doing, and how to best manage the opportunities or the different initiatives to reach that goal are the same.

In today's rapidly changing environment, executives must focus on and manage key variables that affect the likelihood of successfully executing a business strategy. This book will help you do just that by taking you through these eight phases of execution excellence.

"Change before you have to"

— Jack Welch

"I have not failed. I've just found 10,000 ways that won't work.".

- Thomas A. Edison

FAILURE

Most projects, most initiatives, most companies fail to achieve their desired result. That result can be revenue enhancement, cost reduction, customer satisfaction or any other goal. Most of these efforts may achieve a small portion of their desired results or even none at all. And this is because these companies, these organizations, these leaders, fail to fully develop and execute their strategies. Execution is key.

What if your company failed less, and succeeded more? What if you could manage your initiatives to reach your results? What would an extra 10% to 20% increase in performance do to your organization? This is why you should think through how your company can successfully develop a better business transformation process and / or evaluate your current process.

This guide will not provide you every step, every detail. What it will do is help you understand what's important; what you should focus on. I've included sections at the end of each chapter to provide you with key questions to ask, common pitfalls and examples. I have also provided a journal at the end to allow you to reflect on what you've learned to assess your current process and assist you to develop, manage and execute better.

We all want to be the greatest; the best. But what if we just started by being better? Better than what we were yesterday; better than what we were last year. And if we're going to improve the results every day in every way, what could we accomplish? Let's succeed. Let's not fail.

EXAMPLES OF FAILURE: SEARS AND TOYS "R" US

Sears is a good example to learn from. They failed to transform and chose to stay the same. They continued to sell marginalized products at marginalized prices to a population that changed. They were no longer selling in small cities to people on the outskirts. They were selling to people in the cities with options. Their inability to read and adapt to the terrain resulted in its failure. This is almost identical to Toys "R" Us.

Who's going to be next? What do you need to save your enterprise?

Andrew "Andy" Grove, one of the founders of Intel and the CEO who helped transform the company into the world's largest manufacturer of semiconductors, is famous for saying "Only the paranoid survive." The paranoid view everything as a threat.

- Competitors
- Partners
- Customers (changing needs and requirements)
- Internal company capability
- Unknown and unseen new entries to the market

The paranoid seeks to develop plans to survive for each possible perceived eventuality. I am not asking you to become a paranoid executive, but I am suggesting you develop a continual transformation mindset as a way to develop strategies and plans to survive in a rapidly changing business environment

If channeled correctly, this constant oversight can be used to transform your company for the better.

CHAPTER 1: GAP ID

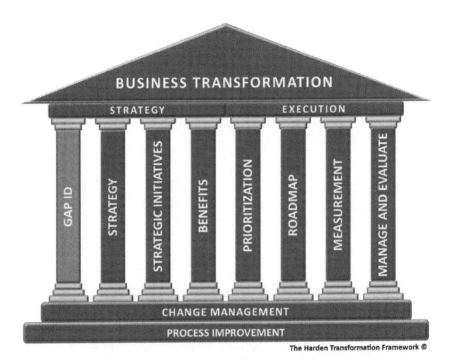

"The more gaps a leader can bridge, the more significant influence she or he can make."

- Pearl Zhu, Digital Gaps: Bridging Multiple Gaps to Run Cohesive Digital Business

GAP ID

CONFIRM AND ARTICULATE THE GAP

It all starts with identifying the gap. The distance between strategy and results is where the performance gap lies in your organization. This makes identifying the gap, or the "Gap ID" phase as referred to here, a crucial kick-off point towards effective execution within any organization.

DEFINITION

A gap is basically the difference between your current situation and your desired situation. A gap analysis is needed to help your business identify how far you have come towards reaching your goals and how far you still need to go to attain them. The objective is to develop a concrete strategy to close any existing gap by outlining what the gap constitutes and what factors contribute to it.

IMPORTANCE AND BENEFITS OF IDENTIFYING GAPS

Identifying the gaps within the organization is the first step towards improving inefficient business performance. The idea is to enable effective execution of a strategy. Without identifying the gap, you cannot ensure the optimal allocation of the relevant resources.

Many, if not most, companies perform below their potential due to the misappropriation of resources and/or lack of capital, appropriate technology or strategic focus. When a well-thought-out gap analysis is conducted, such inefficiencies are highlighted allowing the leadership involved in the Gap ID process to make the most effective improvement recommendations.

When done right, identifying a gap enhances a company's performance. It sets the basis for creating higher quality products and services with increased profit potential. Decision makers in charge of strategic execution are armed with the measurement of resources required for the organization to achieve its desired results.

TYPES OF GAPS

The key question for leadership is "What is the Gap?" The answer starts by understanding the different types of performance gaps that may exist in an organization.

There are four broad types of gaps which can have further subcategories:

1. **Performance Gap**: Expected performance – actual performance.
2. **Product/Market Gap**: Projected sales – actual sales. Do you have the right products / services to meet the right market need? Remember, many market needs may not be within your strategic focus. You can't be everything for everyone.
3. **Profit Gap**: Targeted profit – actual profit.
4. **Manpower Gap / Workforce / Skillset Gap**: Required number and quality of workforce. The required resources with the required skill sets. This can be an actual strength of the organization or it can be a key hinderance to success.

5. **Sales / Revenue Gap**: Forecasted sales vs actual sales

While gaps number 2, 3, 4 and 5 are relatively self-explanatory, performance gap requires a little more detail. The performance in question can be of various kinds. Here are some types of performance areas where gaps can be identified:

Strategic Performance

Includes improvement in brand enhancement, business growth, and market reputation.

Operational Performance

Includes product turnover, cycle time, inventory, and orders.

Customer Performance

Customer satisfaction, customer retention, and market share.

Circling back to the question *"What is the Gap?"*, the management of a company should be able to clearly define and articulate the current gaps in the business they are seeking to manage / mitigate.

For instance, within the product/market gap it can be the number of items sold, or the profitability of the products sold, or the combination of the sold products. It can also be related to the cost of marketing. Sometimes the sales channels are different and resellers use different selling methods. All these factors might be contributing to the gap in question.

Consider a situation where sales are down in the current year compared to the previous one. Further analysis might show that while overall sales are down, profitability is up as a result of the company selling more profitable items. Sometimes the sales might be down, but instead of being down across the board they are down only in a specific segment or region. The company may be facing particular competition in these regions or have poor resellers. Confirming all this requires management to ask more detailed questions to identify the deeper issue.

"**Between *where you are today and where you want to be lies a gap. That gap is the price you have to pay to get to the top.***"

— *Oscar Bimpong*, host of "The Platform," a Radio Talk Show on Fire Live Radio.

SITUATIONS WHERE GAP ID IS NEEDED

You may need to conduct a gap analysis in numerous situations on both micro and macro levels. Here are some examples:

- Developing a plan to improve market / industry relevance / performance
- Improve business credibility to clients and partners
- When an organization is trying to determine the changes needed to become a leader in their market/industry
- Determining requirements to enter a market
- Improving department productivity within individual business units
- Developing and implementing a strategy to acquire / retain specialized resources
- Developing a strategy to improve technical capabilities and -processes (business profitability system, implementation of predictive modeling, customer data modeling, cloud-based technology)

Of course, the list is endless. But the ones listed above illustrate how diverse the situations can be where it is crucial to identify the gaps within an organization.

HOW TO IDENTIFY A GAP

While there is no universal formula for identifying gaps and the process carries different details depending on the strategy, here is an effective framework you can consider:

- Where are you going = what is your desired future state?
- Where are you now = A fact-based assessment of the current state of the business
- What is the Gap = what is the delta (difference) between your current and desired performance?

The company should;

- Review the strategic objectives in question
- Compare them against existing data points
- Use KPIs to compare the difference

Basically, you are calculating the difference between existing and intended results. You can see examples of these in the four types of gaps listed earlier. In other cases, the gaps are not so black and white. For instance, it's easier to spot a gap when you compare $20 million of actual sales to the estimated $40 million.

But some other non-tangible gaps have their own set of symptoms, which management can use to identify them. Here are a few signs of such gaps:

Signs of Gap in Strategic Planning

- Confusion regarding allocation of resources
- Forecast vs actual variability
- Lack of synergy and alignment between business functions

Signs of Gap in Expertise/Knowledge

- Product development performance gaps
- Project performance gaps (missed timeliness and budgets)
- Increased dependence on outsourcing of skills that are critical to business strategic success
- Increased consulting costs

Gap in Management Expectations and Objectives

- Boardroom disagreements
- Lack of motivation among employees
- Creation of factions within the organization

Gap in Corporate Identity

- Decreasing brand awareness
- Diminishing customer satisfaction
- Poor results from marketing efforts
- Low Social Index performance

Culture Gap

- High staff turnover

- Recruitment issues
- Declining employee engagement

As you can see, sometimes determining the gap is simple arithmetic. Other times it is a lot of meetings, questions and analysis.

TOOLS FOR IDENTIFYING GAPS

There are several tools at your disposal to identify gaps. Let's look at a few of the most effective ones.

SWOT Analysis

The SWOT (Strengths, Weaknesses, Opportunities and Threats) analysis technique can be used to identify gaps in performance within an organization. By identifying the gaps in this way, the company can define the ideal solution by capitalizing on their strengths, apportioning resources accordingly while circumventing potential threats.

Here's how this technique can be applied through a quick exercise which can be utilized to perform a high-level SWOT:

1. Establish the reasons why the SWOT analysis is being performed and what outcome is expected from this exercise
2. List all relevant stakeholders who will contribute to the analysis and invite them to the process
3. Utilize a 2 x 2 table, labeling each section as 'Strengths', 'Weaknesses', 'Opportunities' and 'Threats'
4. Brainstorm with your SWOT team, asking members to list the following as related to their desired outcome:
   o Internal factors:

- [Strengths] Positive and strong internal characteristics which help in achieving the objective
- [Weaknesses] Elements that reduce the chances of accomplishing the objective

  o External factors:

  - [Opportunities] Situations or elements that make it easier to achieve the objective
  - [Threats] Factors that can jeopardize the successful achievement of the objective

5. Document the responses then review and prioritize the current gaps that need to be addressed
6. Evaluate the gaps to determine the best way to leverage the strengths and opportunities while minimizing the impacts of weaknesses and threats

Data Analysis Framework

A high-level visual analysis framework is a useful method to provide individuals with specific financials or key metrics in a visual manner to more easily communicate business performance gaps.

Spreadsheets analysis is often the primary tool for illustrating performance gaps. They can provide a quick executive glance or they can be incorporated into data visualization tools (i.e. PowerBI or Tableau). The primary goal is to present the performance gap in a method that is easily digestible by the leadership. This is important to reduce the primary management issue of attacking the data instead of focusing on resolving the issues at hand.

At a minimum, the data should compare current performance to desired performance. The difference in a performance gap should be represented as a total and a percentage difference (for example, $1,000,000 vs $1,500,000 is often not as powerful as a

50% increase). If possible, provide a comparison data with key competitors that can assist in clarifying the importance of the gap to management. Providing the impact of reaching the desired state of revenue, profit and/or market share can also facilitate the discussion related to the importance of the gap.

"5 Hows Questionnaire"

The 5 Hows questionnaire is designed to deliver specific details of how management can solve a particular problem related to identifying and bridging gaps. All questions are directed towards team members who are part of this process. To implement this technique, you need to:

- Define the desired outcome and ensure all team members understand it
- Ask the members how they will accomplish the desired outcome. Kick off a brainstorming session that allows for cross-checking and validating the members' answers
- Once you get the initial responses, ask the same question **4 more times**. Note every subsequent answer and use it as the basis for the next "How".

The repetitive questioning allows you to drive to a deeper explanation and reveal more specific methods to achieve the desired outcome. It also reveals the tasks and activities required at the root level. You can also go beyond the initial 5 Hows if you feel you are not digging deep enough to identify the fundamental tasks.

You must ensure you have relevant information, statistics or other details. Superficial answers are not to be entertained. All relevant team members who have access to the necessary information must be required to engage in this process.

Fishbone Analysis

Commonly known as the cause and effect diagram and the Ishikawa diagram, Fishbone Analysis is an effective root cause analysis technique. It operates on the cause and effect principle, with every correct action bringing an organization closer to the desired effect.

You can apply this technique for gap analysis in the following way:

- Write the desired outcome at the head of the fish,
- Facing right to left, list the chief activities or features needed for partial accomplishment of the desired outcome. Write the activities at the end of each rib in the fishbone diagram
- Take the activities/feature (effect) one by one and analyze the sub-activities/tasks (cause) required under it. Write these on the branches of each respective rib.

Similar to the 5 Hows Questionnaire, this analysis can be utilized with a team session that will allow for cross-validation before finalizing the key findings.

Fishbone Analysis: Example

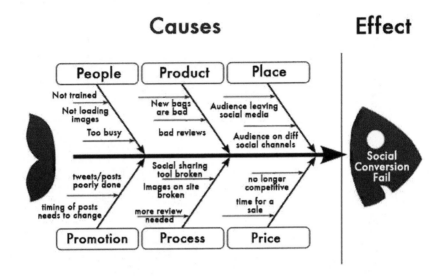

McKinsey 7S

The McKinsey 7S framework is used to identify aspects of an organization that are meeting expectations. By using this framework, you can examine the characteristics of a company through the lens of seven elements:

1. Strategy
2. Structure
3. Systems
4. Staff
5. Style
6. Skills

7. Shared Values

For each of these elements, you will fill in a current and future value. This will reveal any gaps that might exist in the organization. Ultimately, this allows the company to roll out a targeted solution for filling the gaps.

TWO QUESTIONS

It is important to not lose sight of the basic goal of identifying a gap which is to ask the upper management two fundamental questions:

1. Where are we now? Who are we now?

2. Where do we want to be? Who do we want to be?

This is the crux of Gap ID. The better answers to these questions, the clearer the understanding of the gap and the higher the chances of bridging the gap.

"Bridging innovation gaps is a strategic imperative for business execution."

— *Pearl Zhu*, Digital Gaps: Bridging Multiple Gaps to Run Cohesive Digital Business

APPLE'S IPHONE GAP IDENTIFICATION

There are plenty of real-world examples where companies have identified gaps internally as well as in markets. A stellar example is that of Apple.

In the 1990s, Steve Jobs was back at the helm of Apple that was within inches of bankruptcy. He killed most of the products and focused on a few core ones. This was a perfect example of identifying gaps within the company. Fast forward a decade and the company identified a gap in the cell phone market, ultimately revolutionizing the industry with the iPhone.

Even after the initial launch, many labeled the touch system as a passing fad. The results spoke for themselves, quieting the critics, and Apple became the market leader.

Of course, the superb gap identification enjoyed the follow up of an incredible strategy and an equally brilliant execution of that strategy (product performance, customer engagement and support services).

Here are some questions related to the world's biggest corporations and gap identification:

- Why does Amazon want to own a grocery chain?
- Why is Google launching home smart devices?
- Why did Toyota launch Lexus?
- Why are premium and basic TV networks (HBO, Showtime, CBS) creating online channels to separate from cable?
- Why are cable companies getting into the home security business?
- Why did Blockbuster not switch to online movies sooner?

EXAMPLE: GAP ID

Company:

Venture Capital Backed Software Company

Situation:

The company had launched a new software solution focused on Fortune 1000 companies. The strategy to grow was focused on developing strategic partners to assist sales and services related to implementing the solution.

Complication

The market for the services was growing and new Silicon Valley startups were entering the market along with major service providers announcing the development of similar services. As a result, the company was having difficulties developing strategic partner relationships and new customers. Therefore, the need to create alternative sales opportunities to support the business became critical.

Transformation:

The business and technology team assessed the business gaps through the following:

- Current customer needs were determined via interviews and workshops.

- In addition, non-customers that had solicited support in the past, but did not meet prior business requirements, were interviewed to gather additional information related to their needs.

- The technology team reviewed the applicability of the current technology solution for other potential business options.

- Internal challenges and barriers were also identified and assessed.

- Business and service risk were included to provide a complete picture of the business opportunity and challenges.

As a result of the steps above, the company developed a list of unfulfilled solution needs for targeted Fortune 1000 customers and a new group of product and service offerings tailored to the needs of middle market companies, online businesses and startups. A gap to opportunity matrix was created to identify potential business opportunities to close the gaps and support business growth.

The executive team reviewed the proposed opportunities and developed a new business strategy to align with identified business and customer needs. The new strategy included new technology business requirements, a change in the partnering strategy and the need to acquire tangential service providers.

How it was accomplished

The company worked with current customers, potential customers, sales, technology and external resources to assess issues related to customer buying decisions. The engagement of internal experts in the area's business development, operations, marketing, technology and strategy provided the company with great insight into partner decisioning process.

Gap ID Keys

- Continually assess the market for new needs that are not being met by our products and services.

- Assess competitor position to determine potential risk to your business. What are they doing differently and why are they doing it?

- Interview customers to determine if your current products and services are meeting their current and future needs.

- Interview customers and internal resources for their ideas related to acquiring your product and / or service

- Interview customers and internal resources related to tangential services that can provide additional value

- Include individuals from across the company to provide a holistic view of product / service challenges and gaps

- Utilize external resources / experts to provide an outside view of where your product and services can be augmented

KEY QUESTIONS: GAP ID (IDENTIFYING INTERNAL AND MARKET GAPS)

The process of identifying gaps is the key step in the transformation process. The results will determine how you decide to steer your company for years:

Questions to Identify Internal Gaps

1. Where are you currently?

2. Where do you want to go?

3. Why do you want to become X?

4. What do you need to become X?
   - Technology requirements
   - Resource requirements
   - Business capability requirements
   - Business culture requirements

5. What are the chief hurdles to becoming X?

Questions to Identify Market Gaps

1. Do you have a customer council to review your products and services? How is it utilized?

2. What share of the market can you conservatively take?

3. How well does your product/service matrix fit into the market?

4. What has made you successful or unsuccessful in the market?

5. Who are the existing market players and why do consumers buy from them?

6. Are new entries in the market reducing your market share and/or pricing ability?

7. What gaps (product / services / pricing / customer accessibility / partnerships) allowed new entries into your market?

COMMON PITFALLS: GAP ID

Here are some important notes on the common pitfalls regarding identifying gaps that every executive should keep in mind during the Gap ID phase:

The process is too complex

Gap analysis is a crucial starting point. It should not be a substitute for more detailed analyses that may be required at later stages once the relevant project/change has been initiated. Utilizing an overly complex process will limit the ideas generated. This is the ideation, not the evaluation phase. The purpose is to generate as many ideas as possible.

Single analysis framework

Make sure to utilize more than one tool (listed previously) to obtain information and then combine the results. This delivers a holistic view of the gap's scope. Additional analysis can lead to the identification of supplemental opportunities.

Lack of insightful data

Wherever possible, data should be quantifiable. E.g. "15 market growth" instead of "significant growth" or $50 million in business opportunity" instead of "a considerable revenue increase." More data allows you to compare more areas of your business to your competition.

Focusing on the wrong things

During information collection, the focus should be on internal and external business analysis, supporting workflows, and processes

that can have significant impact to the business. Th
time to focus on minor enhancements.

Lack of a clear direction

The desired result should always be carefully and clearly defined.
Without a clear direction, execution challenges or failure should
be expected. Leadership should provide guidance on the relative
importance of revenue growth, profitability, customer growth
and other key performance measures.

LECTION OPPORTUNITY

>erformance relative to this Business

Current Challenges

Goals to Improve Performance

Key Actions required to Improve Performance

CHAPTER 2: STRATEGY

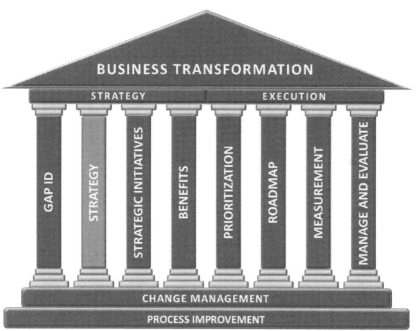

The Harden Transformation Framework ©

"Perception is strong, and sight weak. In strategy it is important to see distant things as if they were close and to take a distanced view of close things"

— Miyamoto Musashi,
Legendary Japanese swordsman

STRATEGY

CONFIRM THE COMPANY STRATEGY

After the organization's gaps have been identified by the leadership there is a need to develop the appropriate strategy or strategies to mitigate the gaps. This chapter will serve as an introduction to the next chapter about strategic initiatives. For now, the focus remains on the big picture and on what is the big answer to the big question: How do you fill the gap you discovered during the Gap ID stage? Let's start with a simple definition.

WHAT STRATEGY IS

"Strategy is a pattern in a stream of decisions."

— *Henry Mintzberg*, Canadian academic and author on business and management

A strategy can be defined as a structure to make decisions about how you will manage your business with the purpose of achieving your long-term goals. Within the context of this book, a strategy is the overall direction a business has to take to bridge the gaps it has identified.

Your strategy is a framework that will guide numerous decisions across the organization, aligning various resources to close all gaps in question. A good strategy will keep your company from running in too many different directions, squandering profits and spreading confusion across different departments.

WHAT STRATEGY ISN'T

One of the biggest problems some organizations have is that they confuse strategy with planning. Strategies and plans are not the same thing. This misconception is a common reason why strategies often are unsuccessful and miss the mark.

A strategy doesn't always answer all the questions required for implementation. That's planning. What a strategy does is clearly establish the rules of the game you will be playing and how you can expect to win. Just as importantly, it also identifies the games you will not be playing; focus is key.

A WORD ABOUT FOCUS

As you take the next step towards filling the gaps in performance (or other categories) you identified earlier, focus becomes your best friend. A well-thought-out strategy helps you focus and prioritize the things that matter.

Remember our Apple example from Chapter 1? They benefited greatly from Steve Jobs' laser-sharp focus. According to Jobs, focus is not about saying yes to the most important thing, but rather saying no to everything else at that moment. If you want to fill the gaps you have identified within your organization, you will also need to encourage a culture of focus.

GUIDELINES ON CREATING A WINNING STRATEGY

COMMIT TO AN IDENTITY

Instead of blindly chasing growth, focus on what kind of company you want to be. This clarity will help you fill performance and other gaps more quickly. Staying true to your value proposition ensures a high success rate when going after your big goals.

CONVERT STRATEGY INTO MANAGEABLE INITIATIVES

Determine which capabilities are actually aligned with your strategic goals. Strengthen and bring them together instead of shooting for erratic "functional excellence." Different departments, units and teams across your organization may not be great at everything. By breaking down strategy into small initiatives, you will drive efficiency across your organization. We'll cover more on this in the next chapter.

AVOID OVER RE-ORGANIZATION

The quest to fill performance gaps and remove the space between strategy and results often leads to over-reorganizing. It can be tempting to shake things up. You need to avoid the endless, unnecessary shuffle of people, processes and systems. Constant, unnecessary or uninformed change can create more issues and lead to overkill.

EYES ON THE FUTURE

This book is not a crystal ball, nor does it promise you one. What you ought to know is your strategy should reflect your ability to re-imagine your company's capabilities, and even create a place for them in the market if possible.

A bold strategy covers gaps by getting in front of change. Don't be afraid of what might happen and innovate out of that anxiety. Your strategy needs to find the middle ground between standing still and changing directions without a clear plan. Just like utilizing a map to get your destination, having a clear path to the future makes it easier for you to align your organization's resources.

"The essence of strategy is choosing what not to do."

— *Michael Porter*, Harvard Business School Professor

MORE GUIDANCE, LESS GOVERNANCE

There's a fine line between guidance and governance. Strategy is about the former, not the latter. People in your organization need a purpose and direction. Your strategy should paint a picture for them, showing the way ahead.

Individuals need to be aware that the leadership has identified gaps and are actively engaged in developing plans to mitigate these gaps. They can gain an understanding either through participating in the Gap ID process (via meetings, surveys or a suggestions process) or by being informed of the process and results (based on level and need). They should also be inspired by the big picture of how those gaps will be filled (i.e. the strategy). Alternatively, too much governance hinders effective decision-making which will also make it difficult to bridge the gaps (developing solutions and managing the required initiatives).

"The focus of gap analysis should be getting to the other side. If you bend-over to analyze a gap too long, you'll probably fall into it."

— *Ryan Lilly*, Write Like No One Is Reading

COMMUNICATION IS KEY

Communication is among the chief principles needed to build employee engagement. From findings of the gap analysis to the strategy to fill the gap, all key pieces of information should be communicated across the organization with the appropriate level of detail to the appropriate resource groups. {

Directives will follow in the next phase as strategy is broken down into strategic initiatives. But even as the strategy is formulated, it needs a spotlight in front of the entire organization.

STRATEGIC PLANNING

A key to strategic planning is that it doesn't really stop. It's a process that you must commit to assessing and updating on a periodic basis. Many people develop a plan yearly, but it should be reviewed and updated on a quarterly basis. This means that the plan which was developed should be pulled out, the assumptions and hypothesis need to be confirmed, and the metrics of success assessed. These metrics may include performance on initiative development and cost, financial, marketing and customer impacts.

For a strategic plan to be successful it needs to be utilized. It's like a map. Hopefully you have a sense of direction, but you continue to refer back to the map as there are many places along your journey where you'll be stopped, be detoured, experience challenges and issues and need to go back to the overall plan. How you map out your journey and how that journey should be executed may need to change based on circumstances.

A great example is when a bridge is out of service. The plan might have been to go over the bridge, but that bridge is no longer available to use. Now you have to go back to the map and look at alternatives to get across to the other side to complete the journey.

As mentioned previously, the time and effort focused on the strategic planning process should include leadership, who should give a sense of direction based on where they see the organization headed. It should also include feedback internal and potentially external subject matter experts that can help validate or invalidate some key assumptions that impact the plan or initiatives.

The strategic plan should also be iterative. Many executives want to get through with the plan as quickly as possible with as few people involved as possible. But it really is a process where right individuals (leadership, management and subject matter experts) need to put out ideas, evaluate those ideas and then have those ideas challenged and supported. This helps the idea become more crystal clear.

Consider an example where you're working with a CIO on his plan. You should ask whether the leadership team, in evaluating the direction, initiatives, and prioritization was able to bring in different elements that helped them determine whether:

a) something was needed

b) if it was possible

c) what were the alternatives

d) what were the potential negative impacts of the idea?

This is why feedback is critical. The plan itself should layout the initiatives, timelines, and metrics of success (all discussed in later chapters in the book).

For instance, working with individuals in a corporation, executives will take a 2 to 3-month process to create a strategic plan to merely show the executive team they have a direction. They'll then put the plan back up on the shelf instead of managing through it. This is why you must have a quarterly process to force the review and validation of the plan itself. Management can then make any necessary adjustments. Don't let the plan become a door stopper, book shelf stuffer or a paper weight.

Examples

EXAMPI

operations, support t

How

Company:

Fortune 500 Telecommunications Company

Situation:

The CEO of the company requested the development of a product and service strategy to enter into a new business market. The resulting solutions were expected to leverage some of its core benefits, but they would also require external business partnerships to create a holistic one-stop shop.

Complication

The company's marketing team had spent over ten months attempting to develop a product strategy without success. The complexity of the new strategy and lack of required internal skill sets and cross-functional expertise led to the strategy not being developed.

Transformation:

The team was engaged to develop and finalize the product go-to-market strategy. We brought in experts in telecommunication strategy and business to develop and manage a cross functional team of internal business experts.

The strategy was developed in 30 days and outlined a $200M business opportunity. It included cross organizational business requirements (product, services, finance, marketing, support,

technology) and external partners strategies to
e solution.

t was accomplished

he company engaged experts in the strategic area and
experienced project managers to support the development of the
strategy. As part of the project, the team collaborated with all
relevant internal functional experts (sales, marketing, finance,
human resources, technology and operations) to assess business
challenges and risks. These internal experts also provided
additional options to enhance the final solution.

This solution encompassed the impact on the marketing, sales
teams, operational and installation teams. Also included was the
impacts and risk to individual customers and their companies
along with potential HR responsibilities the companies offering
the service would require. Lastly, we reviewed partner services
that would be required to fulfil customer needs.

The solution represented all of the key elements to develop a
coordinated approach. The team members were also able to
provide cross organization impacts and concerns that would need
to be addressed. The goal was to ensure the strategy could be
operational, successful and sustainable. The strategy in itself
could have been executed without the details of the individual
impacts of process elements illustrated, but the probability of
success would have been negatively impacted.

Strategy Keys

- Clear goal: develop a strategy to provide a specific service
  to a specific customer group
- Engaged all functional groups to assist in the development
  of the strategy

- Develop a comprehensive risk and challenges list to ensure the final solution addresses each before implementation
- Incorporate the finance team to provide credible financial forecast assumptions
- Engaged external partners, when appropriate, to determine how they can support or be impacted by the new strategy

KEY QUESTIONS: STRATEGY

Questions

During the Strategy process it is critical for leadership and their team to set aside adequate time to fully review the questions below and challenge your underlying assumptions:

1. What is our vision for the organization?

2. How is our company going to grow?

3. What should our company be doing more of?

4. What should our company stop doing?

5. Should the company reduce products and / or services?

    a. They may not be profitable

    b. They may be profitable and outside of primary focus

6. Should the company reduce its footprint (contract to focus)?

7. What are the biggest hurdles our company faces?

8. What could disrupt our organization?

9. How can we improve our services/products?

10. How are our customers changing? What could they want in the future?

11. How can we engage and empower the talent in our company?

12. How can we best serve our shareholders?

COMMON PITFALLS: STRATEGY

Reiterating last year's strategy

Just because a strategy worked in the past doesn't mean it will work in the future. Yes, it might work (it could be moderately successful), but that shouldn't automatically earn it a green light. Even if your gap analysis reveals similar goals, you should still assess all alternatives in the broader context of new circumstances.

"Insanity: doing the same thing over and over again and expecting different results."

— *Albert Einstein*, German Physicist

Complicating it

Just because strategy is formulated in the highest echelons of a company doesn't mean it has to sound complicated. The best strategies are simple and can be easily communicated to all stakeholders. They are succinct and therefore easily implementable.

Ignoring the customer

No strategy is complete without addressing customers and their needs. Here are some questions that should be addressed with your strategy:

- What is your target market?
- Are you targeting a certain segment?
- Are you focusing on a particular demographic or geographic region?
- What do you know about the potential consumers?
- How do their needs relate to your value proposition?
- Are you solving any problems for them?
- How does your product or service create issues for your customers?
- How can the above issues be addressed / minimized?

Ignoring competition and market trends

As with customers and their needs, you need to ask some important questions related to your competitors and market trends:

- Who are your main competitors?
- How is their service offering different from and / or similar to yours?
- Have any new players entered the field recently?
- How have the new players positioned themselves with the market?
- What has been the response of customers to this new competitor?
- Why are customers responding favorably / unfavorably to this new entrant?
- What lessons have you learned from observing this new entrant?

You should also evaluate wider market trends. This will help you spot important themes, shifting expectations and, of course, new opportunities.

Not getting stakeholders on board

Your strategy won't be successful if you don't get key individuals to embrace it and activate it. And how can you get anyone behind it if they weren't part of it? Of course, not every individual will be part of the gap analysis and strategy formulation. You want individuals to feel that their concerns were addressed. You don't want the impression that only a small group of individuals were involved in developing the strategy and expect everyone else to support it.

Lack of planning - how to deliver the strategy

Just creating a quantifiable and streamlined strategy as a solution to the gap is not the end goal. The goal is to fill the gap and to develop an achievable plan for delivering your strategy. You should look inside your organization and evaluate its core skills and capabilities. You need to determine if you need to hire new talent, find partners or engage consultants to support the strategy. The plan will entail many elements that assist in facilitating the strategy's execution.

Overlooking the numbers

You have to get all relevant financials right up front as you chalk out a strategy. Goals for revenue and profit should be mapped out in a way that ensures adequate cash flow for covering ongoing costs. You need to confirm you have the funds set aside for executing the strategy or your strategic initiatives / goals may never be reached.

Not monitoring and measuring progress with the appropriate metrics (KPIs)

Every strategy requires clear goals and milestones that can be measured by metrics. You need to define your key performance indicators, establish a process and ensure you have a system to monitor them. A significant portion of your strategy's success can be tracked and monitored if the right metrics, systems and processes are set up in advance.

"However beautiful the strategy, you should occasionally look at the results."

— *Sir Winston Churchill*, British Prime Minister during World War II

Not guiding the strategy by data

A lot of companies fail to capitalize on big data with regards to their strategy. You should consider investing in business data strategies such as transactional data, monitoring in-store traffic, evaluating online marketing analytics, etc. which can help you record and analyze data. This will deliver invaluable insights that can then be used to build a better strategy and manage the subsequent execution plan.

KEY QUESTIONS:
STRATEGIC PLANNING

As you're assessing your current company, you need to ask several questions about strategic planning:

1. How often does your company develop a strategic plan (yearly)?

2. What is the strategic planning cycle (12 months, 18-24 months, 3 - 5 years)?

3. How often is the plan reviewed by the management team? Quarterly? Yearly?

4. How is the strategic plan communicated to senior leadership and management team?

5. How is the strategic plan communicated to the individuals who will be tasked to implement the strategic plan and fulfill the requirements and goals within the strategic plan?

6. Are there metrics put into the plan to assess its success?

7. Is the plan a living document? Or is it created once every couple of years just to satisfy management's desire to have some measure of focus?

8. Who owns the strategic planning process for your organization? Is it individuals within business units? Is it coordinated with senior leadership? Or is a senior executive responsible for aggregating all strategic plans at a certain time of the year?

9. Who is involved in the strategic plan process? Is it executives only? Management teams? Subject matter experts?

10. Do you evaluate the build, buy, partner methodology within the plan to ensure the goals laid out can be attained in the most efficient and timely manner?

COMMON PITFALLS: STRATEGIC PLANNING

There are three main issues with strategic planning that you need to actively avoid:

Wrong people

Are the right individuals engaged in developing the plan? The wrong people for the plan are individuals who:

a) do not have all the knowledge of the enterprise or the cross functional knowledge and support necessary to achieve goals through the created plan

b) have a limited insight into the direction of the company. Without this knowledge, the individual may not have the ability to create an appropriate and actionable plan or they may not have the time to do an adequate job developing the plan

c) might not have the adequate resources that can be marshaled for the research and evaluation to develop the plan.

Wrong timeline – duration for completion

This is when management states it wants the strategic plan to be completed too quickly. There are always time demands in business but moving too fast can lead to mistakes. Adequate research on important elements like the company's current state, the changing environment and competition may not be possible in the shortened timeframe. However, a rushed plan may not be sufficient for managing the operation going forward.

"Be Quick but Don't Hurry"

- John Wooden, Legendary Basketball Coach

Wrong frame

Strategic planning at the wrong time can also pose problems. The planning process is often mixed with the budgeting process. As a result, management is developing their budget while developing the plan, which can be both a pro and a con.

> The pro: you've developed a plan and by understanding what your true funding needs are for supporting the plan, you can request the relevant funding.

> The con: instead of looking at the overarching plan, individuals become focused on trying to acquire the budget. This may drive them to minimize the size and scope of the plan to capture funding. It may also lead individuals to use the planning process to support the initiative funding in the future.

JOURNAL: REFLECTION OPPORTUNITY

Review your business's performance relative to this Business Transformation Pillar.

Current Strengths

Current Challenges

Goals to Improve Performance

Key Actions Required to Improve Performance

CHAPTER 3: STRATEGIC INITIATIVES

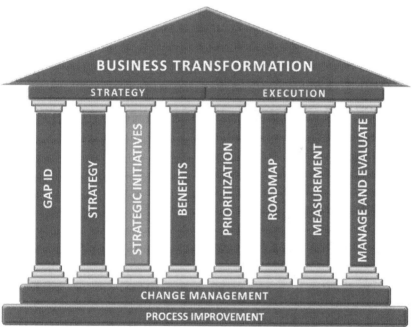

The Harden Transformation Framework ©

"Strategy without tactics is the slowest route to victory, tactics without strategy is the noise before defeat."

— *Sun Tsu, 6th Century BCE Chinese Military Strategist*

STRATEGIC INITIATIVES

CONFIRM THE COMPANY'S STRATEGIC OBJECTIVES

So, you have identified the gap, and crafted a strategy that will fill that gap. But you are not quite ready for execution. First, you need to identify the specific objectives related to achieving the strategy by breaking it down into manageable strategic initiatives.

These initiatives come out of the strategic planning that you started in the previous phase. They are essentially the top priority items that your company wants to accomplish to achieve its goals. The process of prioritizing these top initiatives will be discussed in the Prioritization phase.

For instance, if you want to increase your revenue by 10% or your profits by 20%, you will need to develop operational initiatives to realize these goals. You will probably have several strategies that will require management to be actively involved to turn them into reality.

How will this be achieved? Typical options may include:

- New products / services
- Increasing sales
- Increasing prices
- Market expansion
- Business acquisitions
- Operational cost reductions

- Improved business efficiencies

Once you have identified your strategic goals, you can develop strategic initiatives to eliminate the gap. You need to make sure you have an effective governance and project process to manage and track these initiatives.

You need to ask, "What is the management process by which the strategic initiatives are managed and supported?" Often, strategic initiatives are pushed back to be managed by business units. However, these units may not have the adequate level of project support, oversight or experience to manage these strategic initiatives in an effective way.

YOUR STRATEGIC PROGRAM OFFICE

The initiatives need to be evaluated at the executive level. Therefore, you need to create or have in place a Strategic Program Office that can help to fund, track and evaluate the status of the initiative on a monthly and quarterly basis.

This management and tracking methodology will allow you to quickly determine if ongoing funding should be provided or reallocated to another initiative waiting for funding. You need a governance process that utilizes a stage-gated process or a partial funding process so strategic initiatives can be identified, evaluated, and accelerated as required.

If additional support or management insight is needed, it can be orchestrated from the Strategic Program Office. The primary purpose of this office is to improve the organizations capability to evaluate, start and manage new strategic initiatives as they are reviewed from the pool of initiatives.

The Strategic Program Office should not just be a place where reports are read. Rather, it should be a team of individuals whose purpose is to provide the necessary detailed oversight of these initiatives. Otherwise the program will be seen more as punitive than supportive.

"Plans are only good intentions unless they immediately degenerate into hard work."

— *Peter Drucker*, Management Consultant, Educator, and Author

Perfectly Aligned

It's important that strategic initiatives are aligned to support the corporate direction, vision, mission and goals. These initiatives can include revenue and profit enhancements, cost reductions, customer satisfaction and engagement initiatives, and efficiency improvements.

Improving a company's business situation, financial position, and mitigating its performance gaps requires initiatives in many different areas.

Cost Reduction

Often companies develop profit strategies based on reducing costs. These initiatives can focus on staff reductions, process improvements, facility / space planning reviews, and / or product or service reductions.

Branding

Branding can incorporate strategic initiatives focused on enhancing business value and ensuring customer have the full understanding of product and service benefits.

Marketing

Marketing and social media efforts are another area where the strategy will be broken down.

Personnel

This is especially important where a gap in skills has been identified. Developing and / or acquiring new talent can be critical to business performance. In addition, companies are often simply in need of a general work force to accomplish its goals.

Technology

Strategic initiatives may also require technological and infrastructure upgrades. These may make the strategy execution more capital intensive but enhance business capabilities. The initiatives can also be focused on reducing operating cost related to business activities than can be automated.

Evaluated for Impact on Organization

Strategic initiatives need to be evaluated based on their ability to impact the organization. The impact can be financial (e.g. higher sales) or non-financial (e.g. enhanced business capabilities). As you are fleshing out strategic initiatives, don't lose sight of why you are doing it. Impact and practicality are the criteria by which you have to judge each initiative as it is conceived and developed.

Burdensome Evaluation

This is a common pitfall. Although you want to fully assess the impact on the initiatives, you do not want to make it a burden that cannot be accomplished. Some initiatives may not have enough readily available data to predict an outcome. You want an evaluation to tell a story as to why it should be implemented and the positive impacts it can have on the company as a whole. You do not want to hamper individuals or business units ability to provide strategic ideas because it will be too difficult to provide overly detailed evaluation. You want the evaluation to be directionally correct; an understanding that may require additional analysis for initial approval or ongoing funding.

Use all relevant information so you can prioritize the strategic initiatives (more on that in Chapter 5). You might begin with 50 initiatives which may then be streamlined to just 20. Communicate openly and often with everyone involved in this process. All invested parties should be kept informed throughout the process to understand the decisions and enhance their ability to provided additional initiatives in the future.

Clear Prioritization

You need to be clear on the prioritization process you use. Is it a combination of financial and non-financial elements? Are you weighting the initiatives based on the level of accuracy created through the evaluation process?

You also need to consider whether you use the benefits of one initiative to fund others. If this is a goal, you will need to develop a process to stage initiatives to support the funding of other initiatives. For instance, let's say you have 10 strategic initiatives that you want to drive forward. Five of them will cost you $50 million, three of them will cost you nothing (their cost will be offset), and two of them can help you save $75 million. How are you utilizing the cost saving initiatives as an additional funding mechanism for your more expensive projects?

When you are looking at this prioritization as a funding mechanism, your perspective of the initiative will change. You may begin to think of initiatives based on resources that can be brought to bear in the right way to obtain their expected benefits.

In the end, no company has unlimited resources, including people, time or money. This underscores the importance of prioritizing the initiatives to get the biggest bang for the buck so to speak.

Often, companies look at self-improvements and costly upgrades as being the primary way to increase overall performance. However, that can be too expensive based on impact to quarterly or annual financial performance data. Although this can be true, the management should weigh the initial investment against acquiring the systems or processes via an acquisition. An acquisition may provide immediate efficiencies, save time and reduce risk.

For instance, switching over IT systems often seems to be risky and time intensive. But the long-term benefits of the switch may save millions of dollars. Management should have this foresight and invest in such upgrades or acquire these benefits despite any initial impressions that the effort is too capital intensive.

Of course, having said that, if a corporation does not have available resources, risk profile or funding, they can continue to put off the same investment for years at a time.

ISSUES WITH IDENTIFYING STRATEGIC INITIATIVES

You may face several issues as you are breaking down the strategy into smaller initiatives. How well you deal with them will determine how well you are able to transform the strategy into results.

Initiatives become tactical

It is imperative that the initiatives are at a level which cannot be described as tactical. Strategy is the name of the game thus far. Avoid the temptation to jump to tactics. To an extent, the urgency of transforming strategy into tactics is understandable. But experienced executives know how to operate at the strategic level even as they break down the strategy into more manageable initiatives.

Over-assessment

Don't burden the management team to develop overly detailed valuations right away. When initiatives are over-analyzed, you may be left with just two alternatives instead of ten initiatives. Therefore, you will not have a great pool of ideas as you gear up for execution later.

Support requirements

You need to be aware of the kind of support the initiatives require from across the organization (e.g. finance, sales, operations, marketing HR, IT). Failure to recognize these requirements will create significant problems with execution later in the process.

Ensure the company has the right people with the right skills who can help with the evaluation. For instance, don't just leave it to HR to assess their initiatives. Provide supporting resources (finance, operations, etc.) to review and validate.

Funding

You need to set aside a large enough pool of resources for evaluating and funding strategic initiatives on an ongoing basis. This pool of funds and related projects should be actively managed to ensure coordination and benefit realization and must be a potential redirection of funding.

Culture

Interestingly, perhaps even ironically, successful strategies emerge from organizations which have a culture that accepts failure as part of the process. Not every initiative will succeed and that's okay. If a company does not embrace the idea that everything will not always be successful, you will encourage leadership to avoid developing and recommending ideas they are not 100% confident in. This will reduce the strategic initiatives your company will have access to.

On one hand, you should not be complacent in your evaluations. On the other hand, you need to entertain the possibility that some initiatives won't work out. This realization should also drive you to embrace phased funding as resources are allocated based on success at different points.

Tracking

Make sure you have the right tracking programs in place to monitor the success of your strategic initiatives. Otherwise, you won't be able to identify the ones that are bringing your organization closer to its objectives.

The tracking of success should be identified early in the process. The initiative success metrics and process to acquire and track these metrics must be created prior to starting. Without these metrics in place, initiatives could be simply reviewed based on the project plan completion and budget. Although these metrics are critically important, they may not show the value / benefit expected or will be realized by successful completion.

Project support

As the strategy is transformed into initiatives, you need to rally relevant expertise. For instance, HR and marketing have great ideas which can help the overall company. This could also include IT and business development people. But they may not have the skills set in place to be able to optimally lend themselves to the strategic cause. This can be outsourced to an internal strategy or project team working with company subject matter experts or consultants. Be careful not to outsource too much of your strategy because you can lose in-house knowledge going forward.

TIPS FOR EFFICIENT STRATEGIC PLAN IMPLEMENTATION

Focus on the most important initiatives

The adage, "if everything is important then nothing is." works well here. Don't be overwhelmed by the long list of strategic initiatives. You will learn more about prioritization in Chapter 5.

Galvanize exclusive teams for each initiative

Create cross-functional teams comprised of both specialists and operational staff.

Prepare strategic initiative team leaders and hold them accountable

You need to ensure the team leaders don't simply return to their normal day jobs after developing the initiatives; they need to follow through on all their new responsibilities related to the strategic initiatives.

Don't take on too much simultaneously

Whatever your ideal capacity is, make sure you figure it out and don't exceed it. New initiatives can be activated once earlier ones have been completed or additional resources need to be acquired internally. They can also be activated using outside consultants to support capacity increases.

Stick to the plan

Avoid temporary distractions that can steer you off track and keep you from implementing the strategic initiative. Often what happens is that initiatives are not halted or canceled; they just stop receiving attention and resources.

Operationalize every strategic initiative

You need to see beyond the various reports and recommendations and focus on the results. This requires you to operationalize your initiatives, moving them from theory to practice, and provide the business support to move the performance needle of your organization. Leadership visibility can help focus management to complete and operationalize business initiatives.

Monitor performance

Clarify the Key Performance Indicators (KPIs) and assess them on a monthly basis. This was discussed earlier and will be included in the Metrics / Measurement chapter. Lack of monitoring the right metrics is common initiative issue.

GOVERNANCE (PROJECT OVERSIGHT, MANAGEMENT AND TRACKING)

Strategic initiatives need the right structure and governance processes in place to actively manage the project. It requires the appropriate reporting process to measure metrics of success that are truly important to the project. Therefore, you need the right level of executive engagement to ensure the projects are being managed effectively.

Also, the governance management leader / group / committee must have the authority (either delegated or through leadership position) to challenge the assumptions of progressor the need to continue the project, to allocate additional funds and resources to the project, and to approve potential reallocation of funding and resources to other initiatives.

Sometimes strategic initiative executives have difficulty reporting a status that is not green or successful. They often will not provide a status update that is yellow or red. This challenge creates the necessity to have the right metrics so you're not measuring and reporting project tracking elements, initiatives, activities or tasks as green but are not truly representative of the necessary progress for success.

I have seen many situations where executives and/or project managers only report green. There was once a team of executives that managed their strategic initiatives in this manner. They would create and report on tasks that were small enough to show progress even though the projects were not successful. Once the new metrics were put in place by the governing body to track real progress, many of the project status updates were actually yellow and red. These managers assumed they could catch up later in the process to become green.

As a result of this type of reporting manipulation, executives then wonder why it wasn't reported earlier. Reporting concerns early allows management to provide additional support (funding, resources, etc.) to enhance the projects to properly evaluate the projects ability to meet the expected benefits / goals. If they determine the project can no longer meet its goals / benefits, the funding and resources can be quickly reallocated to other projects.

EXAMPLE: STRATEGIC INITIATIVES

Company:

Fortune 500 Financial Services Company

Situation:

The company was having difficulty generating transformative strategic ideas. Their management team was extremely conservative and focused on meeting financial expectations while minimizing downside risk. Because of this conservative nature they did not promote a culture which valued unorthodox ideas. Therefore, the resulting business initiatives were rarely unconventional.

The company had also allowed individual business units to manage their initiatives. This approach had created issues with generating strategic initiatives, getting them vetted, valued, approved, properly managed and tracked.

Complication

As market growth slowed and competition in their footprint increased, the company required more out-of-box thinking. Unfortunately, the organization's leadership team did not have experienced project leaders that were accustomed to developing business cases for the big ideas and managing their associated risk. The process was further complicated due to the lack of governance and absence of support business tools and processes.

Challenges:

- Executive governance process
- Initiative review and approval
- Business case requirements
- Prioritization
- Funding allocation / reallocation
- Ongoing monitoring

Transformation:

The team developed a "big idea" program for the client to illicit big ideas from their business leaders. The executive program was created to incent individuals to be open-minded and receptive to more radical ideas. The new strategic initiative processes increased the speed of initiative development, review, approval and funding. A governance process, business case tool, and supporting processes were created to support the program.

How it was accomplished

The project support and finance teams were engaged to support the business leaders to create business cases and project plans which met the needs of the governing body. The process was explained early and individuals were available to reeducate new participants. These processes and tools were developed to help the leadership team with a full understanding of their needs and issues. As a result, the business team's positive response led to over $300M in additional revenue opportunities.

Strategic Initiative Keys

- Provide tools to assist with the review and approval process
- Develop a process to allocate funding

- Include executive leadership in governance program to speed decision making
- Support the owners of the strategic initiatives with experienced project managers that are not within their organization to ensure reporting accuracy and transparency
- Allocate funds quickly
- Manage the efforts frequently to provide support

KEY QUESTIONS:
STRATEGIC INITIATIVES

Here are some questions that will help you assess how well your strategic initiative management process currently works:

1. Do you have an active list of strategic initiatives, along with their costs, from the planning process?

2. Are these issues evaluated in financial and non-financial terms to help with prioritization?

3. Do you have the support of your organization in place?

4. Do you have the support and resources to help actualize the idea to fruition?

5. Is there a culture in your organization that allows you to think big?

You also need to ask some questions to review your current strategic initiative program office:

1. Is there are a program office currently in place that is reviewing strategic initiatives on a monthly basis?

2. Are executives engaged in assessing the current status of these initiatives?

3. Is funding available to support the initiatives throughout the process?

4. Are resources available that can be quickly galvanized to assess or assist the initiative if it's not tracking correctly? E.g. can you bring on additional financial resources, project management resources, technology resources, etc. to support in managing the effort?

5. Is the program office, if applicable, viewed as a supporting organization whose charter is to help you succeed or is it viewed as an organization that's just reviewing the status?

6. Do you believe the executive team is adequately informed and knowledgeable to be able to help guide your efforts?

COMMON PITFALLS: STRATEGIC INITIATIVES

Choosing too many initiatives

You may have dozens or even over a hundred strategic initiatives as you break down your strategy. It is quite tempting to launch all or most of them in the hopes of getting the best results. But this is often not practical and drives up the volume of work much beyond the organization's capacity, ultimately hampering numerous processes. Poor prioritization often leads to this problem.

Not providing initiative leaders any incentives

Ideally, your initiative leaders will be your organization's high achievers. But these individuals will be involved in numerous day-to-day business processes. When they are faced with managing a strategic initiative or managing a competing issue related to a day-to-day task, they will lean towards the latter, unless you incentivize initiative management.

Not providing adequate resource support

As mentioned earlier, not all management leaders are prepared to manage projects. Providing project support to help management focus on issues, monitoring progress, and seeking the right support to escalate issues is imperative. This should not be seen as a weakness of a leader, but instead a method to help them manage what's important in their strategic initiatives because they also have a business unit, group, or function to manage.

Avoiding issues

Issues are inevitable and avoiding them only adds to the problem. Often, problems are not reported to the management until it's too late in the execution phase for effective resolution or damage control. You need to encourage the raising of issues as soon as they emerge. This will give you the most options to resolve them and lead to better execution of the initiative and overall strategy.

Not utilizing the team properly

Pursuing strategic initiatives can be daunting. Before you launch an initiative, a company may loop in the expertise of its board members, executives and a bevy of external consultants. But often, key personnel within the organization are overlooked. These can range from subject matter experts relevant to the initiative to technology management responsible for developing the solution. Companies should include the appropriate individuals as early as possible to provide insight into the potential challenges with operationalizing the initiative so they can create alternative solutions. Companies must also establish a two-way communication channel to harvest their wisdom for superior execution of the initiative.

JOURNAL: REFLECTION OPPORTUNITY

Review your business's performance relative to this Business Transformation Pillar.

Current Strengths

Current Challenges

Goals to Improve Performance

Key Actions Required to Improve Performance

CHAPTER 4: BENEFITS

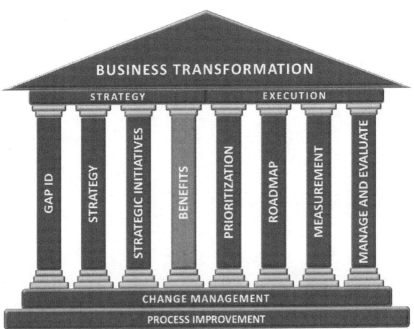

The Harden Transformation Framework ©

"Checking the results of a decision against its expectations shows executives what their strengths are, where they need to improve, and where they lack knowledge or information."

- Peter Drucker, Management Consultant, Educator, and Author

BENEFITS

UNDERSTANDING THE BENEFITS OF STRATEGIC INITIATIVES

This is a good time to reiterate the overarching theme of this book (i.e. filling the space between strategy and execution). A big part of doing this is staying focused on why the strategy was created and what will be the improved status of your company as a result of successful execution of that strategy.

At this point it's critical to clearly understand the expected benefits of every strategic initiative. How well you do this will determine how well you execute your strategy and realize those benefits.

Benefits Realization

As part of the strategic initiatives process, you will clearly identify the benefits to your actual initiatives. These benefits may be financial and/or non-financial. Ideally, you would have been specific enough in identifying those benefits upfront. Moreover, you should also have identified the key metrics for determining the success of the initiatives, both during and after the transformation effort (i.e. service and product development and launch). The values of elements such as revenue, cost, customer loyalty, and customer satisfaction must be quantifiable.

It's no longer acceptable for a company to simply launch a project or initiative, run it through its lifecycle, and then move on to the next initiative. Stakeholders want to know whether or not the initiative delivered the benefits that were expected from it.

There is an increasing importance of benefits realization management, which in our context is the process of identifying benefits of the strategic initiatives. This helps ensure that these benefits are realized and sustained through focused actions and implementation.

THREE REASONS YOU SHOULD IDENTIFY BENEFITS

The initiative was taken because of the expected benefit

First off, the strategic initiative was only implemented because there was a benefit attached to it. This is why it receive funding and was prioritized through the initiative planning process. Therefore, it is a critical goal to ensure those benefits are realized.

You also need to have some level of understanding of what action to take if the initiative is not realized. For example, do you continue with the transformation initiative (i.e. new product) or discontinue it? Or do you modify the initiative in an attempt to improve the likelihood of realizing the benefit. Companies must also ensure an appropriate level of funding available to support the strategic initiative after it is put into action. The initiative might need additional marketing, resources, and technology support as it is developed and implemented.

Better expectations in the future

Secondly, it will help you better set expectations in the future and allow you to make better decisions with new initiatives. Your organization will improve at defining expected benefits as you determine what went right and what went wrong. For instance, did you assume customers would respond in a certain way? If they didn't, why not?

This analysis of success and failure will facilitate the internal learning of your organization, helping it become more prepared to deliver its own services. For instance, you may identify that your company is great at customer service but bad at technology development. In that case you may need to outsource the development, bring in additional resources with the right skillsets, or consider developing partnerships.

Resources constrained

Thirdly, consider the fact that companies are constantly resource constrained. Therefore, it is in an organization's best interest to become more efficient at realizing benefits that can then be allocated to subsequent projects. So, if an initiative is planned to realize $2 million, a portion of those funds can be used to fund future initiatives as well.

Quotes

A project is truly successful only if it delivers the benefits an organization envisions.

Author unknown

BENEFITS REALIZATION MATURITY

Your organizational performance should include its benefits realization maturity level. This measures the percentage of initiatives that were completed on time, within budget, and which defined the goals identified at the onset. Effectively implementing strategies is connected to an organization's ability to deliver successful projects.

BENEFITS REALIZATION MANAGEMENT

Initiatives, projects, portfolios – they can all be aligned to the organization's central strategy through Benefits Realization Management (BRM). However, doing so intimidates many executives. This is because there is no single, universally acceptable BRM process that can be followed.

Having said that, bolder and more innovative organizations are establishing procedures to identify benefits and monitor their progress. The increased focus on topics like benefit realization, executive sponsorship and talent management shows that an increasing number of companies are recognizing the connection between strategy implementation and business success.

APPROACHES TO BRM

There are four main approaches to defining Benefits Realization Management. The first one is to consider the BRM as a change process that affects the organization. As such, it will be defined as the process that organizes and manages initiatives in a way that the potential benefits from the success of those initiatives are actually realized.

The second approach views BRM as a single process. In this case the BRM is defined as the recognition, definition, planning, tracking and ultimately realization of the expected benefits.

The third one is applying the concept of BRM on a project management level. The benefits management process includes the initiation, planning, organization, execution, control, conversion and support of the transformation to realize the expected benefits.

The fourth definition views BRM as a collection of processes designed to close the gap between strategy and execution, by implementing the most important strategic initiatives.

Roles and responsibilities as well as processes, deliverables and principles should be clearly defined in your BRM. The main role is that of a Business Change Manager (BCM) who helps the Benefits Owners (the major beneficiaries) in identifying, planning and reviewing the expected benefits.

The BRM helps the organization maintain a benefit focus as it executes one strategic initiative after the other. A benefit can be described as a measurable positive impact of change. On the flip side, a dis-benefit is a measurable negative impact of change.

Effective benefits realization management utilizes relevant measures, accountable personnel and proactive managers.

Here is what your BRM process can include:

- Identifying investment outcomes
- Defining benefit measures for every outcome

- Collecting data related to benefits measurement to enable better decision making
- Taking a personalized approach to BRM
- Planning new capabilities required to realize the expected benefits
- Analyze the impact that implementation has on benefit measures, using the analysis for improvement

After the plan is completed, the BRM initiative should maintain its capabilities and benefits realization.

PROACTIVE MANAGEMENT

Proactive management is necessary for a benefits-driven change. You need to identify the required benefits and ensure the initiatives are optimized to achieve them. You also need to monitor the KPIs that forecast the benefits delivery.

Engage Managers Early On

The managers in charge of implementing the strategic initiatives are perfectly positioned to bring the efforts to fruition. As such, they should be engaged early on in the process as the benefits are analyzed and projects are aligned with the overarching business strategy.

This will enable the managers to focus on creating business value instead of having a constricted emphasis on the initiative/project deliverables to go beyond the traditional measures of success.

An Iterative Process

You need to understand that benefits management is an iterative process. This usually includes five main phases:

CREATING THE BENEFITS MANAGEMENT PLAN

This includes setting out policies for KPIs, roles and responsibilities, measurement and priorities.

Identifying and structuring the benefits

Various sources are used to collect the requirement. The benefits depend on the outcomes' achievement and management needs to understand the relationships between these by using benefits maps (discussed later in this chapter). You need to document the benefits (and dis-benefits) in terms of value, timescale, ownership and priority.

Planning the benefits realization

This includes agreeing on targets and baseline measurements to identify the existing performance so management can measure improvements. The plan will show timelines and milestones for realizing the benefits. If an initiative has any interactions or dependency on another initiative or process, the plan will reflect that as well.

Implementing the change

Benefits only arise from change, whether it be changes in attitudes or physical changes. As you implement, management should be on the lookout for opportunities to reap additional benefits.

Realizing the benefits

Most benefits will be realized after the initiative has been completed. To ensure that you continue to take advantage of the realized benefits, the change must be embedded into the way people work within the organization.

WHY INITIATIVES FAIL TO DELIVER BENEFITS

A lot of times initiatives fail to deliver benefits. Here are some common reasons why this might happen:

- The focus is on target savings instead of articulating the benefits in a way that can be understood clearly and implemented
- No specific benefits are outlined (Executives may be unaware that the benefits have not been outlined)
- Poorly defined goals
- Too much focus on deliverables or capabilities, which don't result in benefits on their own
- Lack of mechanisms in place for managing the realization of the defined benefits
- Initiatives are often considered finished once their deliverables are complete

Benefits are typically realized over time. Without any structure for managing this key phase, this sometimes results in no one being responsible during the realization phase. That is why it's crucial to clearly identify the benefits early on and assign ownership to the appropriate individuals, including those in charge of strategic planning.

BENEFITS MAPS

Different benefits maps can be created to identify outcomes. These support the agreement of the desired outcomes/results, giving you a birds-eye view of the relationships between outcomes.

There are three main mapping models you can follow: the Benefits Dependency Networks (BDN), Benefits Dependency Map (BDM), and the Results Chain. Let's take a closer look:

BENEFITS DEPENDENCY NETWORKS (BDN)

The BDN has 5 elements:

Investment Objectives

These define the initiative's focus and how it is connected to investment drivers.

Benefits

The advantages or positive impacts to individuals, units or the organization as a whole.

Business Changes

The changes needed within the organization to achieve the benefits.

Enabling Changes

The changes that enable the business changes.

IS/IT Enablers

If relevant, the information systems and technology needed for supporting the benefits to be realized.

BENEFITS DEPENDENCY MAP (BDM)

This also has 5 elements:

Bounding Objective

The measurable end goals that support the strategic vision.

End Benefit

Independent benefits that help achieve the objective.

Intermediate Benefit

Any outcome that a stakeholder considers positive.

Business Change

Any change to your organization or environment.

Enabler

Something your organization creates or acquires to enable benefit realization.

RESULTS CHAIN

This model has four elements:

Outcome

The results your organization is aiming for.

Initiative

Any activity that helps achieve the outcome.

Contribution

A measurable explanation of how a strategic initiative contributes to achieving the goal.

Assumption

Something that your organization believes is necessary for realizing the initiatives but has little or no control over.

An organization should choose the process that meets business needs while ensuring the necessary elements are readily available to provide the data for measuring and monitoring the realization of benefits.

EXAMPLE: BENEFIT REALIZATION

Company:

Fortune 500 Company

Situation:

During the annual planning process the company would often receive dozens of requests for business investment. As the company experienced profitability challenges, funding new investments became problematic. There was additional pressure to ensure currently funded and new initiatives would provide expected benefits.

The company requested support in developing a new approach and process to manage benefit attainment.

Complication:

Unfortunately, the company did not have process and tools in place to capture and track these benefits. In prior years, the company had challenges with simply documenting the expected benefits of each opportunity. The management team had previously allowed the strategic investment to be included in the strategic plans as part of the overall unit business priorities. These investments could request additional resources (HR, technology, etc.) to support the investment, but were not required to provide anticipated benefits for the particular investment. They were only required to state that the investment was needed to reach their financial performance goals.

The individual teams had not utilized financial managers in the past to develop their financial models for individual initiatives. This lack of engagement lead to questions related to the assumptions behind the expected benefits.

Transformation:

The team implemented a new process to review the benefits associated with strategic initiatives. As part of the process, the initiatives were required to document benefits in both financial and non-financial categories prior to funding approval.

Financial Benefits:

- Revenue
- Profits
- Payback period
- Internal rate of return

Non-financial Benefits:

- Customer value
- Strategic Importance / relevance

The new processes provided leadership with multiple benefits to track during and after implementation. In addition, initiative owners were required to review progress toward benefit attainment as part of the ongoing financial reporting process.

How it was accomplished

The leadership created a process to assess the benefits, invested in developing a financial tool to capture the financial and non-financial benefits information, and utilized experienced financial officers to develop and review the benefit models. Incorporating financial managers into the process provided a consistent reporting process and ownership. As a result, leadership was able to review and track benefits on an ongoing basis.

Benefit Realization Keys

- Create a process that requires benefits (financial and non-financial) to be provided with strategic initiatives
- Provide tools to assist with the review and approval process
- Utilize experience resources (strategist and financial officers) to assist in developing benefits
- Manage the efforts frequently to ensure benefits are being tracked

KEY QUESTIONS:
BENEFITS REALIZATION

As you go back and assess your organization to identify the benefits, there are 10 things you want to be able to determine:

1. Do we have a benefit realization process?

2. How often does the company review the benefit realization of individual initiatives?

3. Are there any status points to review support needs to assist projects ability to realize their expected benefits?

4. Are the benefits realized invested back into company profits, set aside in a fund for future initiatives, or available for the responsible business unit to utilize at their discretion?

5. How do you track the utilization of realized benefits?

6. Does the BRM process have additional funding to support other ongoing efforts?

7. How does your organization marshal resources to support projects that may be off-course on their benefit realization plan?

8. Are projects that have expected benefits which are not yet realized canceled or halted?

9. Are such projects allowed to continue? If yes, why?

10. Is there an internal learning process around business realization?

Pitfalls

COMMON PITFALLS:
BENEFIT REALIZATION

Lack of detailed benefits

Companies receive initiatives with either vague benefits (improve sales growth) or wide ranges (between $20 and $50 million over 2 to 3 years). Without clear and detailed benefits, it becomes extremely difficult prioritize, track and evaluate the initiatives. Companies may only include high-level benefits or simply include the benefits (combined with other continuing business operations) as part of reaching the business targets.

Lack of a clear timeframe

Leadership should provide a clear timeframe for benefits realization. Initiative managers must understand if the benefits are expected in year 1, 2 or 3. Without this understanding, issues can arise with future project funding. As a result, business benefits are often not provided on quarterly or annual basis

Lack of a tracking process

Many institutions do not have a process to review the attainment of benefits. Although businesses have processes to manage the status of their projects, they have often neglected to define a process to measure and manage the realization of the anticipated benefits.

Not canceling projects

Typical institutions are not experienced with tracking and canceling projects based on benefit realization. Most business and functional groups have not been required to track benefits at a detailed level and therefore their individual success data has not been available for management review.

Business culture

The culture of the company may reward success but not reward learning from failure. As a result, leaders may not want to provide negative benefit realization results. Fostering this type of culture will not only hinder tracking of success, but also reduce a company's ability to provide additional support to achieve the benefits.

JOURNAL: REFLECTION OPPORTUNITY

Review your business's performance relative to this Business Transformation Pillar.

Current Strengths

Current Challenges

Goals to Improve Performance

Key Actions required to Improve Performance

CHAPTER 5:
PRIORITIZATION

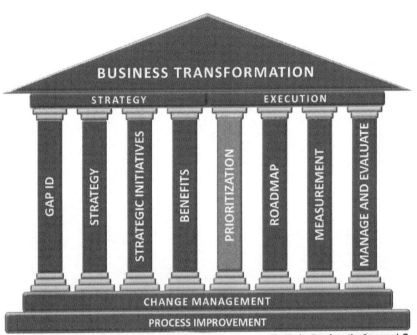

The Harden Transformation Framework ©

"The role of leadership is to transform the complex situation into small pieces and prioritize them."

- Carlos Ghosn, Chairman and CEO of Renault

PRIORITIZATION

PRIORITIZING INITIATIVES BASED ON FINANCIAL AND NON-FINANCIAL IMPACTS

You've identified the gap, established a strategy, broken it into strategic initiatives, and outlined the benefits of each. Now you need to prioritize the initiatives. This prioritization should be accomplished based on their expected benefits and their organizational impact.

You need to compare and align the expected benefits with the internal operational capabilities and impacts of the initiatives. For instance, some initiatives may have great value, but your company may not have the skills (ability, knowledge and or capability) to implement the initiative, at least not currently.

Traditionally, years were spent in planning to roll out all of the priorities in a sequential manner. But in this day and age, you must take a more flexible and agile approach. A prioritized road map will be required. This can be used to see which objectives will provide the greatest overall value (financial or non-financial) and which can contribute value and funding for other initiatives.

"The first thing you must do is decide what you really want. Weigh the costs and the results. Are the results worthy of the costs? Then make up your mind completely and go after your goal with all your might."

— *Alfred A. Montapert*, Author of The Supreme Philosophy of Man: The Laws of Life

STRATEGIC PRIORITIZATION

When we think of Apple's constant upgrade of their mobile phones, they must prioritize numerous features and functionalities. You would have to assume they must leave many items off the final product but have the ability to quickly add other items at the last minute based on changing customer demands and competitor releases. By keeping a constant list of alternatives and their benefits, Apple can release additional features through software upgrades between product upgrades based on what they have prioritized as the most important item to drive revenue and deliver value.

You need to set up a method to prioritize the strategic ideas. Because at the end of the day a company may have many great ideas, but only have a limited amount of funds. There is never enough money to do everything an organization wants to do. And therein lies the rub which is why it's critical to have an agreed upon prioritization process / methodology.

When the strategic objectives are created, you may face different kinds of limitations:

- Limited funding

- Limited resources

- Limited skill sets

- Limited time

- Limited institutional focus

Your organization must do a great job in determining its true priorities. Can one priority fund another priority? Can one priority help the organization faster than the other? Can one be implemented faster? How will you judge a priority that can help the organization today against one that is truly needed in two years?

Having a flexible system allows you to start several priorities at once. If things change quickly the organization can also quickly change from priority one to priority two. You need to have that flexibility in your systems. This flexibility is also needed in the roadmap (more on that in Chapter 6). Ideally, you should have created strategic objectives that can be turned on at a moment's notice or relatively quickly.

The prioritization process should make you think deeply about what is truly a priority. Ask, "What is most important, most critical, and most significant?" It would not have made the list if it wasn't a good idea, but is it a great idea?

Take your organization through the process of listing the benefits, timing, cost, capabilities, organizational ability, and organizational focus. These benefits help sort out the "now" versus the "later" items. The prioritization can be based on need, value, realization, and strategic importance.

"Prioritization leads you to define or redefine task management. Prioritization also helps you build more precise project management."

— *Hugues Franc*, Founder and CEO of Beelev

ORGANIZATIONAL IMPACTS

When implementing the strategy and prioritizing the initiatives, you must determine if the strategy is meant to be: 1) simply incremental, and therefore having minimal impact on processes currently in place (i.e. items to keep the lights on (legal requirements, IT refresh requirements) or 2) meant to be transformational and therefore having significant organizational impact on the people, processes and required structures to be successful. An understanding of these two basic aspects will allow you to develop and implement the operational structure, processes, and to properly align the people to be most successful with a new strategy.

COMMON REASONS WHY LEADERSHIP STRUGGLES WITH PRIORITIZATION

There are three typical reasons why executives and business leadership have trouble prioritizing strategic initiatives:

1. They cannot properly interpret which initiatives are most critical and urgent; they feel numerous initiatives are equally important when they are not.

2. Since they realize they cannot waste a lot of time, they tend to replace the time that could be spent prioritizing with time executing whichever initiative *appears* to be most pressing.

3. They are not good at delegating strategic undertakings to other members of the enterprise.

THE EISENHOWER MATRIX

A popular and effective prioritization model is the Eisenhower Matrix, named after U.S. President Dwight D. Eisenhower. In this matrix-based solution, you will take one initiative and put it in one of the four quadrants:

- Critical and Urgent

- Critical and not Urgent

- Not Critical, but Urgent

- Not Critical, nor Urgent

"What is important is seldom urgent and what is urgent is seldom important."

Author Unknown

As you re-evaluate the situation, you will notice that the initiatives might shift from one quadrant to another.

TIPS FOR EFFECTIVE PRIORITIZATION

Clearly Align Initiatives with Strategy

Underscoring the relationship between the initiatives and overall strategy provides an important perspective to the prioritization process.

Sort Initiatives Based on Impact and Required Resources

The impact and resources can be financial and non-financial. This process is part of creating a culture that understands the importance of prioritization.

Foresee Roadblocks and Potential Setbacks

You should know the cost of delays, understand the resources needed for an initiative, and also have a contingency plan in place.

Start with Time-Sensitive and Highest Impact Initiatives

Swift analysis is needed to identify the most time-sensitive initiatives. Encourage management to kill or pause initiatives without substantial value for your business.

Don't Overburden Your Team(s)

You need to be mindful of an initiative's impact, and of the resources required to execute it. This will help you avoid going beyond your team's bandwidth.

Keep the Customer First

It's easy to lose sight of the customer during the "introspection" as you look within the company for enhancing execution. So keep asking which decisions will have the most positive impact on the customers. This will always lead to superior prioritization.

Delegate Effectively

The relevant people at your organization need to understand the prioritization process to better play their part in the execution. Create and empower a team that you can delegate authority to execute. This empowered team will then have the necessary incentive to assist in prioritization process.

Identify Metrics Crucial for Your Organization

Different metrics are important for different companies. You need to identify the KPIs that matter most for your organization and the individual initiatives benefits tracking as you prioritize strategic initiatives

Balance Service/Product Improvement and Process Improvement

Management is often stuck between adding new service/product features and streamlining processes/infrastructure.

ROIs don't always reveal the best way forward; in most cases the best solution is to manage a bit of both.

Value Projects Important for the Long Term

Often, management also struggles to choose between initiatives with immediate financial benefits and those that create a foundation for long-term success.

Avoid the temptation to always prioritize the low-hanging fruit and give the longer-term initiatives due attention as well.

Dealing with Conflicts and Doing it Together

Prioritization is a lot about dealing with conflicts / competing demands. Management, executives, and other decision makers are under considerable pressure to balance the diverse needs of the company against limited resources.

Prioritizing strategic initiatives requires these decision makers to understand the different needs of the departments and team involved in addition to the costs and benefits of the initiatives themselves.

All relevant parties should understand and accept the process by which initiatives are prioritized. In many cases they will need an explanation of why a certain initiative was considered more or less important than another one. Where appropriate, these individuals should receive feedback on how initiatives were prioritized. This understanding will help manage current and future conflicts.

Focus

At the end of the day, prioritization requires focus. Steve Jobs, Apple co-founder, was considered to be an extremely focused business leader. He clearly illustrated this concept skill when he returned to Apple in the 1990s.

The company was nearly bankrupt before it became one of the most valuable companies in the world. It was also the first company to crack a $1 trillion market capitalization.

Among other things, it was his ruthless focus and prioritization when he returned to Apple (killing off 70% of the product line) that laid the foundation for the unmatched comeback and growth of the company.

Every executive can take a page from Steve Jobs' book to create a laser-sharp focus and prioritize more effectively.

When done right, prioritization improves the strategic discourse at highest echelons of an organization from where it permeates down to the rest of the company. Ideally, the priorities are instilled in the organization's culture.

You need to confirm whether every strategic initiative has been prioritized in the best way for the whole company. Your prioritization ensures the optimal use of the company's resources, current and future. You also need to create options beforehand that should be available in an economic slump. This will provide you with the information you need to change priorities (if at all) in such an event.

Companies are invariably more intricate than any prioritization models or advice might suggest. For instance, the strategic objectives may not be as well defined as you want them to be when you come on board. Other times, there might be a misalignment between the strategic objectives and the departments.

Superior prioritization will help you fill the gaps, fix misalignments and even force management to clarify strategic objectives.

Priorities can also change as you re-evaluate the initiatives after certain milestones. If you manage the priorities properly, you will lay the groundwork for inherently improving an organization.

Of course, you will need the support of the leadership team to assist with making difficult decisions. Successful executives invariably take more risks. They focus on limited priorities and have an excellent idea of not only what is important at the moment, but what will be important after a certain time.

Once you have prioritized the initiatives, you need to swiftly identify the most strategic projects, clarify the priorities to relevant people, and then gear up for measuring the performance of the initiatives.

EXAMPLE: PRIORITIZATION

Company:

Fortune 500 Company

Situation:

In order to properly review, fund and manage new opportunities, the CEO of the company had requested that all strategic initiatives be prioritized based on their impact to financial growth, customer acquisition, strategic relevance, internal operational requirements, and governmental compliance.

Complication

The leadership team had not been required to prioritize strategic initiatives across revenue generating business units and support functions in the past. Therefore, the leadership was unable to provide guidance on prioritization. Also, the company had not previously utilized a quantitative rating process to assist with the prioritization process. As competition became more intense, prioritizing the funding of new initiatives became an urgent need.

Challenges:

- Prioritization methodology
- Leadership involvement and approval
- Ongoing monitoring

- Continual prioritization

Transformation:

The team develop a new prioritization approach All business units were required to provide strategic initiatives (based on size and scope) to a leadership governance body for review and prioritization. The strategic initiatives were then prioritized based on key financial and non-financial metrics. Each metric was given a value to be used in developing a quantitative rating for each initiative. These initiatives and their ratings were then reviewed and prioritized by the leadership team.

The new approach allowed management to implement a process that leveraged leadership experience to give a holistic approach to prioritization. Also, this forced leadership to articulate what was truly a priority for the company allowing management to align their respective functions with the articulated priorities.

How it was accomplished

Leadership and key managers were provided the methodology for prioritization and were engaged in reviewing and approving the final prioritize list of initiatives. New evaluation tools were then developed to assist in the prioritization process.

Prioritization Keys

- Develop and communicate a process for review and prioritization
- Provide tools and experienced resources to assist with developing prioritization metrics
- Develop a process to review the prioritized initiatives
- Include executive leadership in the review and approval of prioritize initiatives

KEY QUESTIONS: PRIORITIZATION

Here are some insightful questions you should use when reviewing your prioritizing process for strategic initiatives:

1. Do you have strategic initiative prioritization process?

2. Is the leadership team engaged in reviewing the initiatives with the responsible initiative owners?

3. Do initiative owners understand the key drivers of prioritization (costs, revenue, profits, strategic relevance) during this review cycle? The drivers may change in during different business environments.

4. What strategic or organizational priority does the initiative support?

5. What are the Key Performance Indicators (KPIs) for the initiative? Can they be tracked?

6. How important is the timing of execution of this initiative on its likelihood of success?

7. How long will it take your team and any external units to complete the initiative?

8. Do you have clear guidelines of success?

9. Is all relevant data available during the prioritization process?

10. Have you considered all opportunity costs?

11. What is your process for revising your prioritized initiatives in light of new information or changing circumstances (internal or external)?

12. Have you considered how prioritizing one initiative affects other initiatives?

13. Are there any disputes among business units regarding prioritization?

14. What process do you have in place to rectify the conflicting priorities?

COMMON PITFALLS: PRIORITIZATION

Every process comes with its set of common pitfalls. As you are prioritizing your strategic initiatives, make sure you are not making these mistakes:

Not giving enough time to prioritization

It can be tempting to jump to executing the initiatives without first identifying which ones deserve the company's resources more urgently.

Not seeing the big picture

Every decision should contribute positively to the big picture (i.e. the strategy the initiatives are supporting).

Being distracted

Don't get bogged down in the process of funding and managing initiatives at the expense of prioritizing initiatives. Stay the course and continue prioritizing tasks based on the KPIs and other metrics you have identified as crucial for ranking the initiatives.

Not delegating

It is critical that a team is created to manage the program of initiatives. This will allow management to delegate to capable resources. Not having the right people to trust and share the work at the prioritization stage will create problems with execution later on.

Ignoring new information

While priorities cannot shift at the drop of a hat, ignoring new information can have negative impacts and be detrimental to individual initiative and overall business success. Not adapting to certain types of new / changing information can create significant issues with execution.

For instance, while you have prioritized optimizing a certain process, more immediate issues may force you to focus your efforts on a different process (business emergencies often take precedence).

JOURNAL: REFLECTION OPPORTUNITY

Review your business's performance relative to this Business Transformation Pillar.

Current Strengths

Current Challenges

Goals to Improve Performance

Key Actions required to Improve Performance

CHAPTER 6: ROADMAP

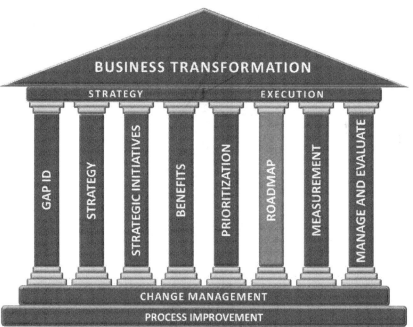

The Harden Transformation Framework ©

"Having no plan is like leaping off a precipice and trying to knit yourself a parachute on the way down."

- Kelli Jae Baeli, Armchair Detective

ROADMAP

Now with the prioritization set, the value of strategic initiatives understood, the tracking system communicated, and the focus identified, the next step is to create the roadmap. The roadmap should be developed based on strategic, financial, and operational needs. It should include properly staged solutions, activities, and projects. Remember that in an agile / flexible enterprise these initiatives may be change or reprioritized at any time.

WHAT IS A ROADMAP?

Your roadmap is your strategic plan which not only defines the desired outcomes but includes major steps and milestones you will need to cross to achieve the outcome. The roadmap should also serve as a communication tool. You should consider it as a high-level document that helps leadership articulate the strategic focus. It helps answer the "what, when and why" behind the overarching goal and your plan for getting there.

Example of Roadmap Information:

- Business Strategy
- Prioritized Strategic Initiatives
- Backlog of business strategies and initiatives
- Implementation timeline
- Responsible business / initiative owners
- Expected business value

The roadmap alone doesn't mean you are at your destination. But it does mean you have taken a big step towards the destination because you now know the way. In order to reach your destination, you need a map to inform your directions. To understand the role of your roadmap, a key thing you must remember is that it was designed as a strategic document. As such, it will not capture each and every detail of your strategic plan. This brings us to another important understanding - knowing what a roadmap is not.

WHAT A ROADMAP IS NOT

A backlog

A backlog is a different kind of document. It is a list of the uncompleted tasks needed to achieve the strategic initiative, arranged according to priority. The roadmap planning process is where high-level strategy is created based on a compilation of backlog tasks and ideas. The roadmap may actually include prioritized and staged backlog items.

A project management tracker

A lot of managers confuse a roadmap with documents that compile the details to complete an initiative. This would include the different activities, people responsible for the tasks, meetings to be held for issues, milestones, deadlines, etc. All these need tracking and updating throughout the process. But all this is not the purpose of a roadmap; that would be the function of a project management tracker.

An Execution Plan

It is crucial that everyone is clear on this. A roadmap is not an execution plan. Rather, it does a great job at showing you what can be achieved within a certain timeframe for the organization to achieve its goals.

Prerequisites for a Good Roadmap

There are two main prerequisites for a good roadmap: good leaders, and well-articulated goals. If you are pushing your strategy without ensuring your teams are emotionally buying into the goals, the roadmap might not get you to the destination you are trying to reach.

You need good leaders that inspire people in your enterprise. They will allow units and teams to do their best, all the while being guided by the roadmap. This empowers them to not only do as directed, but also come up with creative approaches that accelerate the achievement of your strategic goals.

Roadmap Helps Decision Making

Ideally, a roadmap provides a multi-year view of your strategic vision. Roadmaps can also change based on new information. At its core, a roadmap is important because it helps leadership prioritize and make real-time decisions. It is a living document, in contrast to a typical annual plan or a budget. You can update the roadmap as you come across relevant new information so long as the changes are made in a timely fashion and communicated to all relevant people.

Keep in mind that the people connected to the roadmap should understand what the new information and its resultant changes mean, in both the short and long term. The idea is to keep the organization responsive to shifting circumstances. It is not enough to anticipate speed bumps; tools, such as a roadmap, help you circumnavigate such blocks.

KEY THINGS TO REMEMBER ABOUT YOUR ROADMAP

- A roadmap is used for discussing and creating a vision of predetermined and prioritized actions that's shared by the organization.
- The roadmap is conditional. The elements can change based on future events and all users of the map need to understand this.
- A good roadmap includes high-level details. The individual plans contain more detailed elements. The roadmap should focus on the value of initiatives, their timing and resources needed.
- A roadmap clarifies dependencies and therefore enables better planning of the tasks to complete the initiatives.

DON'T EXPECT TO GET IT RIGHT, RIGHT AWAY

It is normal for the first draft of a roadmap to be less than perfect. In many cases, this is essentially the executives' rough notion (initial draft) of how the initiatives will play out in terms of tasks and time.

The Space Between Strategy and Execution | Gregg Harden

You should also not expect the roadmap to be completely consolidated across the organization and neither should you expect all stakeholders to be clear about roadmap instantly. So be prepared to experience multiple rounds of revisions before considering your roadmap as "complete".

Similar to the military axiom, no plan survives contact with the enemy, the best roadmap will need to be adjusted / enhanced after it sees the light of day. New voices can provide additional insights.

ELEMENTS OF AN EFFECTIVE ROADMAP

Vision

Put it on the top of the roadmap. It will serve as a guiding light that shows everyone why they are doing what they are doing.

Values

Your values should align with your vision. If not, think about what needs to be modified to ensure everybody is driven by the same values.

Critical Objectives

These are objectives that must be achieved to turn the vision into a reality and can apply to the organization at large or a specific department or role.

Strategies

Include all the strategies needed to achieve your goals. Think about the desired outcomes and how you intend to reach them.

Tactics

Mention the main tactics and required actions under each strategy. This is what will transform all elements of the map into a reality. Avoid the temptation to breeze past this phase. Think about the actions you need to take. Clarify who is in charge of doing what and the expected time frames. Failure to do so is a leading cause of unsuccessful strategies.

Roadblocks

You will inevitably run into roadblocks. This is why a good roadmap will inevitably showcase potential roadblocks and risks for the strategies and tactics.

Milestones

These will identify important accomplishments throughout the process of achieving the goal. They are also good points at which to re-evaluate and reassess your progress; and if needed, tweak the roadmap. They keep people motivated on longer projects, so use them to track and celebrate progress.

Often management struggles with creating an accurate roadmap because of shifting external forces and internal demands. You should also avoid the pitfall of assuming your roadmap is a guarantee of how things will turn out. While senior management is less likely to make this mistake, meet with all your employees to help them understand it is a flexible tool to guide the company.

By ensuring the strategy is instilled in your roadmap, you can illustrate the importance in its execution. It will also help the individuals involved in implementation understand their value in its execution. This is a powerful way to grow teams, boost their morale and enhance their capabilities. Ultimately, this will improve execution and enable the organization to more easily close the gaps identified.

Finally, implemented correctly, a roadmap functions as a GPS for the organization. It will tell the driver (management) where they are and highlight the fastest way to the destination. It also enhances efficiency by minimizing time wasted on figuring out "what is next?" With the right strategic road map, you can make great decisions more quickly and execute your initiatives and your overarching strategy in a much better way.

"If you don't know where you are going. How can you expect to get there?"

— *Basil S. Walsh*, former CEO of Diageo, the world's largest spirits group

EXAMPLE: ROADMAP

Company:

Fortune 500 Health Care Company

Situation:

While the company was going through a business transformation effort, it identified additional initiatives that would be required to achieve the operational and financial goals of the business strategy. As a result, the company required the development of a strategic roadmap to ensure management's focus on implementing the necessary technological and operational business improvements.

Complication:

The improvements that were required extended beyond internal cross-company improvements and included improvements across external partnering organizations. These external cross enterprise improvements would require sequencing and coordination across both companies to achieve the identified goals. Adding complexity to the roadmap, the funding of the initiatives would be approved by the individual enterprises.

Transformation:

The team worked with transformation teams across both impacted enterprises to develop a comprehensive list of improvement opportunities to support the business strategy. This list of improvement initiatives was reviewed for costs, impact and prioritization within the internal enterprise transformation teams and then across enterprise transformation teams. The cross-company prioritized list was then provided to senior leadership for final vetting and prioritization based on alignment with business goals.

The roadmap included:

- Business Vision

- Initiative alignment to business vision

- Initiative impact on business success

- Timing of initiative implementation

- Internal business requirements to support the initiative implementation

  o Resources

  o Funding

  o Additional pre-work

- Linkage to other business initiatives

- Initiative sequencing requirements

- Internal business needs (Operations, HR, Training, Compliance, etc.)

- Technology requirements to support implementation (technology infrastructure and software upgrades, etc.)

The resulting roadmap provided a three-year view of technology and operational initiatives and how each addressed the areas listed above. This roadmap was reviewed with business and functional leadership to gain acceptance of priorities, resource commitment and timing of the initiatives.

How it was accomplished

The leadership teams of both organizations realized that certain initiatives would require support and synchronization across companies to be successful. They also determined that the roadmaps could not be developed in silos. Leadership also provided clear cross company prioritization. As a result, each organization was able to develop their individual and cross organization roadmaps in a coordinated process.

Roadmap Keys

- Clearly identify business vision and strategic initiative alignment
- Provide an overview of the initiatives that include their impact of strategic vision
- Included prioritized initiatives on a timeline to illustrate the number of initiatives, overlap, and required sequencing and coordination
- Provide leadership with individual and cross-organization prioritized initiatives and their anticipated impacts on strategic vision
  - Include cost, resource needs and sequencing impacts on initiative
- Ensure leadership is engaged to approve the final roadmap
- Review final roadmap with impacted groups to confirm alignment

KEY QUESTIONS: ROADMAP

You need to ask these questions to assess the effectiveness of your roadmap:

1. Is the overarching vision of the roadmap clear?

2. Have you reviewed your values and ensured they align with the vision?

3. Are all prioritized initiatives included?

4. What are the goals that will be achieved by executing the strategy?

5. Have you identified the appropriate milestones with regards to priorities and resources?

6. Does the roadmap take into account resources (internal / external) required for implementation?

7. Does the roadmap ensure the initiatives are not overlapping with competing initiatives and competing resources?

The Space Between Strategy and Execution | Gregg Harden

8. Does the roadmap include costs for each initiative (if applicable)?

9. Does the roadmap include the benefits for each initiative?

10. Have you identified the anticipated challenges / roadblocks to the roadmap (funding, internal capability, change management, business process challenges, timing, prerequisite initiative completion, etc.)?

11. How often are roadmaps reviewed and updated?

12. Are current roadmaps included in business strategy planning for continued relevance?

COMMON PITFALLS: ROADMAP

Make sure you avoid these mistakes when creating the roadmap:

Locking the roadmap

Given the evolving market and unforeseen organizational changes, you should constantly review and update the roadmap based on relevant new information.

Changing the roadmap too much

This is the flip side of the first mistake. If you find yourself changing the roadmap too frequently, chances are you are not making good progress towards your strategic goals. This doesn't include necessary changes related to new and relevant information that impacts the business or the roadmap.

Not involving relevant stakeholders

Having the wrong people involved while creating the roadmap is one of the biggest mistakes companies make when developing a roadmap. Make sure all relevant stakeholders are involved from the beginning because they can provide unique insight, improve execution and enhance the likelihood of initiative success.

Adding too much detail

Incorporating too many details into the roadmap. Include only high-level "stories" for the roadmap leaving the details for the individual plans.

The Space Between Strategy and Execution | Gregg Harden

The roadmap should be communicated to an expanded group that includes leadership. Because their time is often constrained, it should also be presented in a way to ensure it is easy to review. This will allow additional information, insights and suggestions to be gathered.

Neglecting the strategy

You cannot create a good roadmap if it lacks the proper alignment with the strategy. As you plot strategic initiatives and other elements on the roadmap, consistently check its alignment with the overarching strategy.

Priorities overload

Avoid the trap of trying to build a little bit of everything. Poor prioritization will directly impact the quality and efficacy of your roadmap.

JOURNAL: REFLECTION OPPORTUNITY

Review your business's performance relative to this Business Transformation Pillar.

Current Strengths

Current Challenges

Goals to Improve Performance

Key Actions required to Improve Performance

CHAPTER 7:
MEASUREMENT

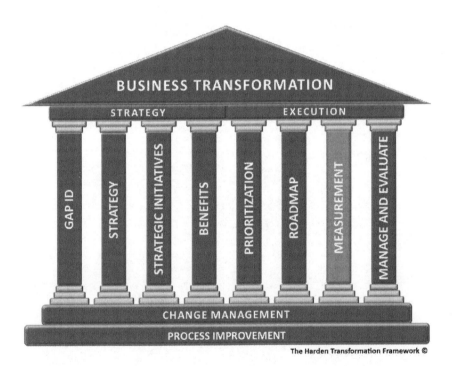

The Harden Transformation Framework ©

"Define clearly how you will measure success in meeting the business purpose and vision."

- Pearl Zhu, digital visionary

MEASUREMENT

Successful business transformation efforts require leadership to clearly determine the focus of change (strategy, products, operations) and identify what success looks like. Moreover, they need to create metrics to assist in the evaluation of success. Therefore, it is critical to develop the appropriate measures to evaluate and track goal attainment.

During the transformation effort, business initiatives should have been identified and prioritized partially based on expected benefits. These initiatives must be continually assessed to review their progress. One of the review metrics should include the benefits expected to result from its successful implementation. Although benefit realization can be extremely difficult, it should the goal.

DATA, MEASUREMENT AND METRICS

When measuring business performance, it's important to understand the differences between data, metrics, and measuring.

- **Data** is a point of information

- **Measurement** is the process by which we aggregate, and review performance based on information

- **A metric** can be on data point or a combination of data points to give a collective view such as housing starts, employment rate, gross national product, and/or market value.

A metric is an individual element even though it may be influenced by many things or by collective pieces of data to create a metric or indicator. It is important to remember that metrics and measurement should be fluid. As an organization grows and prospers, it should constantly look at what new metrics are available to be utilized as a strategy is implemented.

Many organizations spend significant time and effort to develop business cases to illustrate the value of a strategic objective without identifying how they will track the specific success related to this objective. For instance, a company may state that the new system will increase sales associate efficiency and drive improved sales, but they may only have sales as the metric. They often do not have the ability to differentiate what improved sales.

This metric may not be able to accurately identify if the system, a changing market, a price change or new store layout was the driver of the increase in sales. For example, can we accurately determine if the lift in sales was directly attributable to the new strategy; or conversely show that not reaching the sales improvement was related to the market rather than the result of the strategy?

Some more questions you can ask:

- What is the process by which we will track the value?
- Do we have access to the relevant data (timely and accurate) to process the value?
- Do we have a tool for tracking?
- Do we have a system to track it?
- Do we know how, when, and where we will track the value realized from the new strategy?
- Do we need to build something (methodology, tools, systems, processes) in advance to specifically measure and track value / benefit realization?

- Can we show a direct correlation to the implemented strategic objective in the right period or timeframe (for instance, increase sales, improving profits)?

- Is there more than one balanced set of realization metrics that can be integrated?

"What gets measured gets managed."

— *Pearl Zhu*, Author of Digital Master

VALUE REALIZATION AND TRACKING

Understanding value realization is one of the key points for any type of strategic implementation of a process, a function or a technology. How are you going realize it and how are you going to track it? Here are a couple of things you can do.

- Create a list of performance indicators that map back to the strategic objective. They can be revenue, profit, customer retention, customer satisfaction, cost reduction, efficiency improvement, number of calls, number of meetings, number of bids, number of won bids, etc.

- You want to establish a bucket of metrics (typically 5-7). This is not to overwhelm or inundate you with too many metrics. Rather, it is to provide you a full view of the value. Also, by having a balanced set of metrics you have a clearer picture of what is working and what is not. You may see an uptake in sales activity but profit margin decreases. You may see a decrease in bids, but because of a different focus you may see an increase in win rate or an increase in overall revenue. You can get a view of how the different metrics are working in different areas. This may alert you to how the new strategy has been implemented in different areas across states, regions and / or countries.

You need to clearly identify the overall goal and then determine the indicators that will show the goal is being achieved, or at least showing movement / progress towards the goal. Unfortunately, this is not typically identified before the implementation. Companies often attempt to develop the metrics after the strategy is executed. This is especially true for technology projects where individuals feel that it is too difficult to measure success.

THE NEED FOR SYSTEMS, CHECKS AND BALANCES

The challenge is that you may need to build systems, checks and balances in advance to be able to capture and track success. You may not have the information (data) from the past for a baseline, but by taking the time to identify the metrics in advance you will develop a more valuable baseline for apples to apples comparison data.

Moreover, you would have had a longer lead time to determine if the metrics are the correct ones for measuring success and if the data is hard to find. This additional time allows you to determine if the metrics are SMART:

- Simple
- Material
- Actionable
- Reliable

- Trackable

SPECIFIC AND STATIC METRICS

As mentioned above, metrics should be SMART. In the best case, a metric should be specific and static (it can be captured at a point and time). The converse is measurement. Measurement is an evolving process for capturing metrics to enhance business knowledge. Measurement allows for different metrics to be utilized at different times. When measuring, you find specific metrics to give you information at a point in time that's comparable to show progress, growth or success.

MEASUREMENT

But measurements in the process must evolve over time. You may start with a new system measuring usage, which will evolve into measuring performance using the new system. Similarly, you may start with a metric of clicks on the website. But you'll end up moving that metric of success to the sales volume of the visitor, the sale size of that visitor, or the profitability of the individual product. It's imperative that you understand measurements are fluid and must be adjusted periodically as you adapt to how success is rated today vs yesterday.

An example would be using developing and evolving metrics to measure website performance. Potential questions you can ask with regards to the web and metrics are these: Am I measuring clicks? Am I measuring sales? Am I measuring the most probable sales? Am I comparing apples to apples, did I do that before? Am I comparing my metrics against what someone else is doing (a leader in the space)? Am I reviewing and measuring customer satisfaction with what they're buying because they could be buying things 1 and 2, and really wanted to buy 1,2,3,4, but were unable to find them? This is why understanding that the particular measurement metrics can changes is so important.

BALANCED SCORECARD

There should be a balanced set of metrics. For instance, a balanced scorecard that provides you multiple views of what you are trying to measure, including: financial (revenue and cost), company (impact), customer (impact), employee (impact), cultural (impact).

Having a balanced set of measures across multiple groupings allows a clear understanding of the value of any individual initiative. For instance, a new product may not be trending as much revenue as you may have anticipated, but the customer impact of that new product is significant. Understanding that customers value what you launched is important.

- The customer may value what you launched but they just might not need it now. They may have bought a substitute

- Their value may indicate the other customer will purchase the product / service

- The product / service itself may not sell, but its ancillary products / services may be enhanced because this product / service is now available. For instance, offering insurance for a product may increase sales of the product even if the insurance itself it not purchased. Consumers may assume the availability of insurance illustrates the company's confidence in the product / service.

Another example is a product or solution may not be as successful as you want, but the impact to the organization is important.

Maybe the product gives you different insights into the future that you had not thought about previously. Maybe the lessons learned from this new product helps identify additional future customer needs and requirements as they utilize this product or service. Maybe it helps you understand a different category of services or products that you need to be providing.

Conversely, an initiative may be meeting of exceeding its cost reduction metrics, but the impact to the organization might be negative. For instance, the company decides to implement a new sales system that is less costly to operate than the current sales system. But the company may now be experiencing other issues related to the new sales system. There may be issues with the ability to input sales information; the system may have a lag, and / or the data may be corrupted. All of these issues could be hampering the sales cycle. And although the solution may be meeting its metrics (its single metric of success being cost), other negative impacts on the organization are being seen despite its success.

"What can be counted doesn't always count, and not everything that counts can be counted."

— *William Bruce Cameron*, bestselling Author and Columnist

SAMPLE METRICS / IMPACT WORKSHEET

Business Goal: Revenue

Purpose: Measuring the core focus of the business (selling a product of service)

Positive Impact	Negative Impact
Easy to identify	Individuals may focus on the easiest strategies to sell products
	Individuals might focus on low margin Products / Services

Comment:

Must determine if other aspects of sales (margin, overall profits, or focus products) need to be included to focus sales in the areas that matter most.

Business Goal: Profits

Purpose: Product / service profitability. Sales without profits lead to failure of businesses.

Positive Impact	Negative Impact
Sales may only focus on higher profit products / services.	Sales may avoid selling lower profit products and push higher profit product / services that do not solve customer needs.
	Some lower profit products may be the focus on long term growth.

Comment:

This metric should be utilized in combination with revenue.

Business Goal: Shareholder value

Purpose; Ensuring business alignment with shareholder needs.

Positive Impact	Negative Impact
Individuals will make decisions that focus on reaching the goals of shareholders.	Short term desires of shareholder may impact long term strategies for success. Shareholder needs might not always be aligned with customer needs and/or company needs.

Comment:

Short term vs long term strategies and impacts should be communicated in more detail than through measures.

Business Goal: Product Development

Purpose: Ensures new products and features are assessed and developed

Positive Impact	Negative Impact
Product teams will be encouraged to review current products and develop new products and features to meet customer changing needs.	New features or new products do not always lead to sales. Unnecessary product development and implementation can be expensive

Comment:

Companies must have clear goals and metrics to ensure the products developed are implemented correctly.

EXAMPLE: MEASUREMENT

Company:

Fortune 500 company

Situation:

Increasing industry competition led the company to review the profitability of all its business units and products/services. As part of the process, business units were required to develop new activity-based cost for its portfolio of products / services. The company requested support to develop performance measures to better manage the business profitability.

Complication:

The specific unit's leadership team was utilizing metrics that they understood and were comfortable describing. These measures had been in place for years and continued to indicate that they were growing and profitable.

The company's executive leadership team wanted more detailed metrics to confirm the profitability of business unit and how their model growth would impact the unit and the company.

Transformation:

The business analysis framework was designed to provide activity-based costs focused on key business functions (acquiring and managing customers and their products).

The resulting metrics would evaluate accounts based on a number of factors including: the size of accounts, duration of accounts, profitability of accounts, and overhead associated with managing the accounts (customer service, risk management, etc.).

As a result of utilizing new metrics to measure performance, the leadership team was able to determine that the majority of the business units new accounts were not profitable.

How it was accomplished

This is an example of the importance of having the right metrics to measure success. A business process / activity map was utilized to develop process / activity-based costs. These new metrics aligned to individual account profitability. The metrics they had been using were related to portfolio size and new account activation which did not provide profitability data.

The team worked with all areas of the company to develop the cost models and incorporated external resources to review operations and costs across competitors.

Metrics Keys

- Executive leadership strategy was utilized to guide the metric development (profitability instead of growth and portfolio size)
- Metrics were evaluated based on applicability and importance to the business strategy
- Subject matter experts were included to help review current and future metric availability
- A metric dashboard was created to provide timely reporting to the leadership team

KEY QUESTIONS:
MEASUREMENT

You should be asking these key questions to make the most of measurement:

1. What are your strategic goals?

2. Do you have business metrics aligned to your goals?

3. How are metrics utilized (to review results, to provide incentives, to direct changes in strategy)? Each of these have different impacts on individuals within the company.

4. What are you currently measuring?

5. Are these measures sufficient? Do these measures align to your business goals?

6. What are the positive impacts of the metrics?

7. What are the negative impacts of a certain metric?

The Space Between Strategy and Execution | Gregg Harden

8. Do you have a specific business measurement process / group?

9. Do you have predictive metrics?

10. How often are your metrics reviewed for strategic relevance?

11. How timely are your current metrics (today, yesterday, last month, last quarter)?

12. How quickly available are your metrics? Can management access the metrics at any time?

13. Are your current metrics providing useful information for effective management of your business operations?

14. Does your current set of metrics provide you knowledge to act strategically (change business direction)?

15. Do you have a balanced set of metrics (financial, customer, market, employee and partners) that provide a holistic view of your business?

16. Do your metrics have the ability to evolve with business goals and strategies or are they static (the same metrics you have always utilized)?

COMMON PITFALLS: MEASUREMENT

Many companies fail in terms of metrics because they do not identify and articulate the following:

Not defining success

Companies may start a transformation effort focused on growing market share, reducing operational cost and improving customer engagement without defining success. Is success 10% reduction in cost, 5% increase in market share or 20% increase in engagement. Understanding the goals is critical to defining measures.

Identification of success vs. progress metrics

Companies may not determine and communicate what is considered success or what is required to show adequate progress. If companies have broad success goals, they will typically provide less guidance on required progress. Without communicating adequate progress goals, leaders do not have baselines to properly evaluate performance measures / metrics.

Not identifying key business metrics in advance

Companies do not determine all the required key metrics to evaluate strategic initiatives in advance of launching initiatives. Identifying success measures early allows the company to identify the appropriate metrics. It also provides financial management with adequate time to develop the appropriate collection and tracking process.

Confirming applicability and usage of metrics

Companies may not review necessary metrics for availability, accuracy and reliability. Another benefit of identifying metrics early in the process in the ability to test metrics in advance for their applicability and availability. A metric may be extremely useful, but an alternative may be required if it is difficult to obtain and track.

Planning a review process

Developing and maintaining predetermined timeframes for reviewing metrics is key to reinforcing the benefits realization process. What is measured is managed. Management may accidentally create the perception that identifying and tracking benefits is not necessary, or that enough benefits have been realized, if there is not constant oversight management.

Isolating key factors

Companies may not determine how to isolate factors related to an initiative to allow the metrics to be utilized. Sales is a key example of this issue. It is often difficult to track the results of business improvement in sales to a particular initiative (factors could include marketing, pricing, competitor actions, etc.).

Metric Importance

The organization may not test metrics for overall importance. They may exist, but not be important to the current business strategy. As mentioned earlier, measurement teams should constantly review and evolve metrics to be in alignment with the business's strategy.

JOURNAL: REFLECTION OPPORTUNITY

Review your business's performance relative to this Business Transformation Pillar.

Current Strengths

Current Challenges

Goals to Improve Performance

Key Actions required to Improve Performance

CHAPTER 8: MANAGE AND EVALUATE

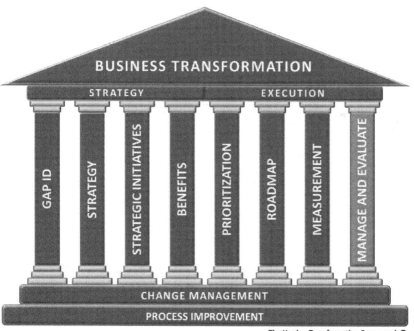

The Harden Transformation Framework ©

"Operations keeps the lights on, strategy provides a light at the end of the tunnel, but project management is the train engine that moves the organization forward."

- Joy Gumz, Project Auditor

MANAGE & EVALUATE

Let's do a quick recap. This is what you have accomplished until now:

1. Identified gaps in your business

2. Created a strategy that will mitigate the gaps

3. Broken the strategy into manageable strategic initiatives

4. Clearly understood the expected benefits of each initiative

5. Prioritized the initiatives based on financial and non-financial impacts

6. Developed a roadmap based on financial, strategic and/or operational needs

7. Developed appropriate measures to evaluate/track goal attainment

The next step is to develop a process to manage and evaluate the launched strategy and strategic initiatives. You have to evaluate how well the strategy has been executed. What you need to understand is that this evaluation is not only an "end of the initiative" – it is a constant process that begins with the launch of the initiative and includes initiative management and measurement. You will be consistently managing and evaluation success while identifying potential course corrections.

Quotes

"Action expresses priorities."

— Mahatma Gandhi, Indian Lawyer, Politician, Social Activist, and Writer

The Space Between Strategy and Execution | Gregg Harden

MANAGING

In order to set up your program office to manage your efforts, ask yourself who will be engaged and what will be their roles and responsibilities. You also need to determine how this information will be communicated back to leadership for review, assessment, approval for moving forward, and how to handle any decisions on shutting down or adding to the budget of a project.

Types of individuals you add

Who do you add? There are different types of individuals who work on projects and programs. There are knowledge experts who know the solution. There are company experts who understand the company and how it operates. Then there are project experts who understand the project.

The most important thing to remember is that managing a project is different than understanding the underlying solution. Many people are put into positions of project management who don't have the skills, background, or the diligence to manage them.

Project management requires not only the skills to review, track and evaluate projects, but knowing how to determine risk, when decisions need to be made, and when a project may need additional resources. The ability to understand how to support a project or initiative through additional management, resources, follow up, or motivation is very important. These aren't always the same skills that knowledge experts have. It's imperative, therefore, to ensure the person managing the project does have them for the initiative to be successful.

"Talent wins games, but teamwork and intelligence wins championships."

— Michael Jordan, considered the greatest basketball player of all time

Roles

It's important that you determine the roles within the project and what they are responsible for on the project. Are they involved in the activities in the project? Are they just to be informed of the project status / progress? Are they simply supporting the completion of the project? Are they actually engaged in making decisions? Are they responsible for the project's success?

To avoid unnecessary structure, use a program with a reporting structure and timeline that safeguards information will flow as necessary to the individuals who help, support, manage and evaluate the project.

Developing the appropriate structure for managing the effort is also extremely imperative. It is critical to ask not only who is involved, but when they're involved? When key meetings will be held and who will be engaged in those meetings? How often will those meetings be held? What information will be shared in those meetings? What decisions should be made during the meetings? Who has approval authority? What is the process for escalation?

The idea is to make the meetings efficient and effective and allow people to actively participate; not simply be seen as a reporting exercise. The purpose of these executive meeting sessions is to engage everyone in understanding what is happening: What issues might be in place? What additional support is needed? What changes should be made to the project to make it more effective? You need to evaluate the benefits and see if they are still attainable. The meetings should review current status, require decisioning and provide insights into the path forward (including potential issues and challenges).

Evaluation

As you're managing the business initiatives you should also ask, "How do we evaluate them?" Often, initiatives are managed through timelines; Are they on schedule? Or on a budget? They're not always managed on benefits realization, so you should manage your efforts based on progress toward the anticipated realization of the benefits. Considering revenue, cost, and performance as part of the initiative management process is critical.

You may decide, based on this information, to change or alter your project in order to focus on gaining more benefits. Maybe it's a different strategy, maybe its different resources. You may also decide to stop an initiative because it may not reach its anticipated goals and shut that initiative down. You may decide to move funding and resources to support another active initiative or consider another initiative awaiting approval and funding. Having a quadrant of metrics (as discussed in Chapter 7) by which to manage and evaluate the initiative as you continue to develop them is also critical.

You will not be able to evaluate all the metrics during the effort. But you may be able to do additional analysis of the market, the solution, and the effort to determine if your initial evaluation or analysis was correct. Maybe some things have changed. Maybe the market has changed, maybe customer desires have changed, maybe your company has changed. Considering these new changes may alter what the initiative can hope to accomplish. It's important that the initiative is constantly managed and evaluated as part of the effort.

You should also assess your team and their capabilities. You have assigned individuals with certain skills to the effort, based on stage and requirement. Evaluate their performance and whether changes need to be made going forward, additional team members should be added or removed, or a new solution or project or team brought in.

EVALUATION TEMPLATE

The evaluation criteria can include the following key items:

- Project status (on time, within budget)
- Expected benefit
- Update anticipated benefit
- Project team evaluation
- Risk to the project
- Cost to date
- Future cost
- Comments section

THE RIGHT MILESTONES AND METRICS

Milestone choices are unique for every organization. These can be anything from a new system launch to rolling out a new product / service and /or hiring key staff. Ideally, you would have picked out the metrics carefully. The right key performance indicators (KPIs) will give you the best insight into the quality of your execution.

Here are some important things you should get right to manage and evaluate your success easily and accurately:

Link them to the strategic goals

While the metrics can be financial or non-financial, you might also use metrics related to sales, marketing, operations, safety and even environmental impact, where applicable. Whatever the case, make sure the metrics are tied to your overarching strategic goals and they move your employees towards the required actions for superior execution.

Keep it simple

Avoid the common pitfall of overloading your staff with excessive KPIs. A rule of thumb is four per department. You also need to train your team on how to track the metrics so evaluation becomes easier, otherwise the data may not be monitored or even updated correctly.

Make sure the data is updated

It is only through up-to-date data that you can perform a meaningful evaluation. Ensure the latest data is not only recorded, but also reported promptly. This also helps you get invaluable feedback on your company's efforts and can highlight problems in advance.

Periodically report the progress of the initiatives to relevant team members and stakeholders. Easy-to-understand visuals will help this effort. The metrics should also be reviewed during follow-up meetings.

"In God we trust; all others bring data."

— W. Edwards Deming, Professor,
Author, and Management Consultant

Ask

In addition to looking at the numbers, you can also evaluate your strategic plan's success by surveying key stakeholders. This includes your employees, customers, and business partners.

From asking specific individuals direct questions to creating an online survey for anonymous responses, you can approach this in multiple ways. The questions will, of course, be unique to the organization. The responses can provide invaluable insight into how the strategy execution is perceive and or valued. If you're getting the kind of responses you were hoping for, it means you are executing your strategy well.

KEY ASPECTS YOUR EVALUATION SHOULD COVER

Your evaluation will cover numerous items related to your strategy. While every metric and aspect are important, a few crucial facets show the big picture. Don't let the bevy of stats and metrics bog you down and keep you from recognizing them:

Internal Conflicts

Internal inconsistencies keep a strategy from being effective. You need to determine if your strategy supports the current structures and policies of the company. Whatever targets are laid out by your strategy, they should align with the overall corporate goals. In the same vein, the strategy's internal elements should not have any conflicts with the internal processes of the organization.

Alternatively, you must determine if your current structures, processes and policies are hindering your performance. The process improvement highlight in the appendix provides additional information related to this challenge. If this is the case, you must evaluate if it is more important to do is as have been done in the past or change it to achieve your business strategy.

External Factors

An effective strategy is also one that matches the environment. This includes customers, competitors and even the regulatory / government requirements. Your evaluation should determine how successful the strategy has been in creating value with respect to the external factors. For instance, did the strategy help the organization match market needs?

Competitive Advantages

The creation of competitive advantages is a hallmark of successful strategies. Your evaluation should determine whether strategic and competitive advantages were created as a result of the successful execution of the strategy.

Feasibility

Your evaluation should also answer the question whether the organization can implement the strategy. This feasibility check determines whether the company has the necessary resources for implementing the plan. It also highlights any issues that you may face as a result of implementing the strategy.

PLANNING AND MANAGING THE EVALUATION

Below are some key items to assist with your evaluation:

Define what needs to be evaluated

- Describe the evaluation program
- Choose a logic model

Create the evaluation brief

- Also known as terms of reference, this includes:
  - Purpose
  - Scope
  - Key Evaluation Questions

Form an evaluation team

- Create an evaluation agreement for internal evaluations
- Create an evaluation proposal and evaluation contract for external evaluation

Manage the evaluation design

- Determine how data will be collected, analyzed and reported for answering the key evaluation questions

Manage the evaluation work plan

- Work out the timeline of milestones and deliverables

Implement the work plan, including production of report(s)

- Create an evaluation report

Circulate the report(s)

- Encourage application of the evaluation findings
- Create recommendations
- Create a policy brief

COURSE CORRECTIONS AND ELIMINATING THE SPACE BETWEEN

Once you have your evaluation findings, you will be able to identify potential course corrections. This identification of potential course corrections brings you back at the Gap Identification stage where you will evaluate any new gaps. You have now come full circle, ideally after solving numerous problems for the organization. During this cycle other initiatives and / or parts of this initiative would have provided unique value (financial and non-financial) to the organization. The best executives take an iterative approach to eliminate the space between strategy and execution.

With each cycle from the Gap ID phase to the Manage & Evaluate phase, the gap is either completely eradicated or significantly reduced. In either case, you can move on to identifying new gaps as you continually refine your business strategy and approach.

EXAMPLE: MANAGE AND EVALUATE

Company:

Fortune 500 Healthcare company

Situation:

The company was engaged in a significant business transformation effort. The program would require the management and coordination of business and technology transformation projects across three enterprises.

The executive team determined that they would need to engage an experienced program leader, with industry and operational experience, and additional program and project support to help manage the transformation effort.

Complication

The company did not have the required skill sets in house to manage an effort of this type of transformation. The size, scope and short time frame also provided significant challenges and put the transformation at risk.

Transformation:

The company engaged experienced program and project managers to assist in the transformation effort. This experienced team of professional were able to develop a program management and governance processes that would incorporate both internal and external transformation projects.

The governance model provided executive leadership with weekly updates on the progress of transformation teams.

The program office created a leadership friendly governance process, and the new governance process implemented the following activities;

- Weekly project status / update meetings at the individual project level

- Bi-weekly program review with senior leadership incorporated into another standing senior leadership meeting. This avoided the need to institute a new meeting with a time constrained executive team.

- A monthly assessment and reprioritization of the strategic initiatives within the investment pool

- A quarterly "continue, go, pause, adjust, or shut down" assessment of initiatives.

This process allowed leadership to:

- Manage and provide funding on a monthly basis to determine if projects needed additional funding

- Determine at senior level what other support was needed to direct the project

- Have a mechanism in place to allow continual management and evaluation

At the conclusion of the first phase of the transformation effort, individual transformation teams provided lessons learned from the project. Each transformation teams (internal and cross enterprise) provided a detailed list of what was done well, what should be leveraged in the future, and what could be improved in the future. These detailed lessons allow the company's program and project teams to continually improve.

- Clearly communicated expectations of the value of the transformation effort
  - These expectations help with decision making during the project
- Internal communications
  - Cross company communications to improve coordination
- Cross enterprise communication
- Improving the usage of change management throughout the project
- Identify and implementing process improvements during the transformation effort
- Financial metrics to track success

How it was accomplished

Executive management was incorporated into the governance process. The team leveraged existing weekly executive meetings to ensure constant engagement and timely access for executive decisioning, when necessary. Also, utilizing a current meeting minimized the challenge of creating an additional meeting for executive teams.

Cross company governance meetings also engaged all impacted parties on the issues and challenges. This approach provided individuals with a method to coordinate their approaches to managing issues and challenges.

Manage and Evaluate Keys

- Develop a governance process to manage the process
- Create a consistent timeline for review and evaluation

- Develop a meeting format that includes leadership and project team leads (as necessary)

- Include only necessary information for leadership review

Provide adequate and timely information in advance for leadership review to focus the meeting on decisions, not updates.

KEY QUESTIONS: MANAGE AND REVIEW

As you ponder how you will effectively reach the results of your strategic initiatives, you need to ask yourself several questions about this process:

1. Do you have a program office process set up to manage your strategic initiatives?

2. Are they incorporated into senior leadership sessions to get the right people looking at the right things?

3. Do you have a process to provide additional funding, withdraw funding, pause projects, stop projects and/or start new projects at the senior level?

4. Do you have continual visibility into the on-going efforts (bi-weekly, monthly, quarterly)?

5. Do you have the right people in charge of the overall program managing multiple initiatives or involved in the individual initiatives?

6. Do you have the roles properly aligned for project leaders (project management knowledge) vs. subject matter experts (business knowledge) vs. corporate experts (internal company knowledge), and are they properly positioned and coordinated with the teams?

7. Do you have an evaluation process to stop or shut down your initiatives / projects instead of simply dying a slow death?

8. What is your process for pausing, stopping, and shutting down projects?

SOME MORE IMPORTANT EVALUATION QUESTIONS

1. How well did the initiatives work?

2. Did the initiatives contribute to the desired outcomes?

3. What unintended outcomes (positive and negative) were created?

4. What magnitude of changes can be attributed to the initiatives?

5. Did any specific elements of the initiatives make a notable difference?

6. How did external factors influence the initiatives?

7. What did you learn from the process (information on customers, markets, internal competencies, etc.)?

COMMON PITFALLS: MANAGE AND EVALUATE

Program Management Office (PMO)

It is critical that a program office is setup to manage and monitor progress before the effort is launched. Incorporating a program office in the early stages of the transformation effort will provide the team with a clear understanding of the business reasons for the effort. This knowledge will assist in the PMO with decisions throughout the program.

Governance

Having a program office does not eliminate the need for a structured governance process. Leadership may create a team to manage the effort but have an appropriate governance process to manage the initiatives. Governance processes critical for oversight.

Metrics

Program offices require data to review progress of business initiatives. This data can include project completion percentages, number of employees trained, number of issues identified, number of system bugs identified, along with others. Not having the appropriate metrics to evaluate initiatives can hamper the programs ability to adequately review and assess progress.

Visibility

Does management have appropriate and timely visibility to key leadership. Leadership's engagement is required to provide guidance and support. It also presents a mechanism to review difficult decisions.

Go - no - Go

Companies should set periodic "go-no-go" project reviews. These reviews require an assessment of the company's ability to meet the expected "go live" dates. These decisions should include all impacted groups. The goal is to communicate challenges and concerns with completing the project as anticipated and the ability to realize expected benefits. It provides a concrete point to stop projects that are not expected to meet their expectations or determine the necessary support to help it meet their goals.

The Right Resources

Project teams have assigned resources but may also need to engage other individuals with key business, process and customer knowledge. It is important that these individuals are identified prior to project launch (additional resource support / insights should be constantly sought by the team). Not having the right individuals involved in the process can lead to project difficulty in the future.

Relevant Experience

As mentioned earlier, projects require individuals with business, process and project experience. Most business leaders have developed skills for managing the business along with their other responsibilities. These managers may not have project management experience. Not having experienced project managers assigned to manage the projects can significantly impair project success.

Escalation

The program office may lack a clear escalation process to manage issues. All projects will be presented with items that cannot be addressed without management support. Having a clear escalation plan will shorten the time between issue identification and issue resolution.

Fear of Failure

It is not unusual for project management teams to be afraid to identify and present issues and challenges. Companies should ensure their teams provide both successes and concerns during status meetings. Teams should understand that shinning a light on concerns is critical to providing support to improve project success.

JOURNAL: REFLECTION OPPORTUNITY

Review your business's performance relative to this Business Transformation Pillar.

Current Strengths

Current Challenges

Goals to Improve Performance

Key Actions required to Improve Performance

FOUNDATIONAL ELEMENTS

CHANGE MANAGEMENT

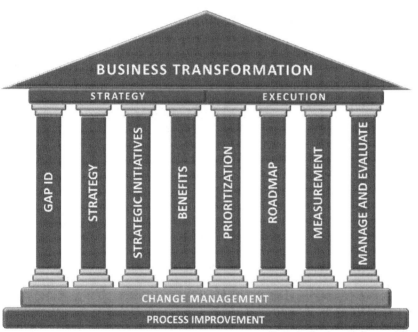

The Harden Transformation Framework ©

"People don't resist change. They resist being changed!"

- Peter Senge, Systems Scientist

CHANGE MANAGEMENT

One of the often-overlooked aspects of business transformation is change management. Change management is often seen as an HR function to ensure people are comfortable with anticipated and unanticipated change. However, when you think of change management in its truest sense, it's determining and managing the impact of change on our employees, our customers and our partners. Understanding the change impact equation is very important to understand the impact of change. This understanding can assist in developing strategies to mitigate potential negative impacts of change on the business transformation effort.

In the past I had the chance to review a rather interesting model on organizational change. It assessed three elements: The Amount of Change, the Speed of Change and the Impact of change when assess and organizations ability to accept change.

Amount of Change, Speed of Change, and Impact of Change

Companies must consider the amount (size and quantity) of change, the speed of change (over a short or long period of time, happening quickly or happening in the future), and the impact of change (significant impact on my ability to complete my tasks or reach my goals). Companies must review amount of change individuals can endure and factor this into their decision making. They need to fully understand the speed / immediacy of the change and the impact of change on their ability to do jobs, complete their roles, achieve their income goals and/or their ability to fulfil their career needs / aspirations.

Companies often relegate change management You need to communicate the direction the company is going in and also help employees, customers and partners understand how the change will impact them along with how you are attempting to manage the intrusiveness and complexity of the change. Lastly, change management should seek to explain how you will provide them with the tools, training and support to effectively manage through the change.

Individuals Impacted: Employees, Customers, and Partners

With that as a backdrop, it is critically important to understand what the groups perceive the change will be. A process should be developed to keep your fingers on the pulse of how people believe the will be helped and how they perceived the adequacy / sufficiency of the level of training and support they will receive.

This is one of the places where companies fall. They assume that because they have communicated and are providing support, and that people understand change is coming, it will lessen the stress. This is not true. The company may be making every attempt to mitigate the impacts of change but if your employees, customers and or partners do not see what it is or trust that it will be sufficient, you'll still create "noise in system" and challenges to successful implementation.

This is extremely important when considering the response of employees during the transformation process. Employees will make their own individual determination on the potential impact within their performance, income, job stability and career opportunities. Managing these individual determinations and the volatility is a primary reason to develop a communication plan early in the process to assist in mitigating potential overreactions and their impact on the transformation.

POTENTIAL IMPACTS OF CHANGE

- Employees: turnover, lack of engagement, lack of support
- Customers: reduction in satisfaction, defections, decrease in customer engagement
- Business and community Partners: turnover, pricing issues, support instability, satisfaction

THE TEAM AND NOT JUST A LEADER

Given the critical importance of successful implementation of a business transformation effort, it is critical that there not just be an individual or team of change management individuals at the Program Management Office (PMO) and not within the working groups. It is important that this role and these plans be integrated into individual work streams and project efforts at the start of this transformation effort.

These groups should identify what they believe is the change management risk and the impacts that they may have on the effort. The change managers should assess the potential responses and impacts (negative and positive) that may arise from employees, customers employees and partners and how they need to best be communicated initially and continually throughout the process.

With this integration into workstreams and the initial assessment they should then begin the communication process and continually follow up with the impacted groups for the workstreams and across workstreams. The change managers should leverage different tools and techniques (in-person meetings, online questionnaires, text surveys) to stay engaged and aware of what is happening, when it's happening and how it's going to impact the groups or the effort. They should continually monitor the impact of the change, and also the impact on the ability of those impacted groups to perform their duties.

Change managers and leaders must understand that employees must feel engaged and support the process to allow it to be efficient. Customers must understand the changes that are coming and be willing to endure it also to get the maximum benefit of the transformation. This is also true for partners. How they respond and support the process also extremely important to the overall success.

As you've probably heard before, implementation does not mean success. To fully realize the benefits of the transformation you will need all impacted parties to:

- Be fully engaged in the process
- Support the change
- Embrace the change

Prepare to go through the change and move forward to help you achieve your expected benefits

EXAMPLE: CHANGE MANAGEMENT

Company:

Fortune 500 telecommunication company

Situation:

The company was seeking to transform its 1,500-member national sales team into a world-class professional sales organization. To support this strategy, the company invested $25 million in new sales support technology to help improve the growth and profitability of the $1 billion business unit.

Complication:

The new sales / lead generation system was extremely complicated to operate, and its login requirements were time intense and inefficient. Therefore, the team did not use the technology, and visibility into the sales funnel plummeted. As a result, sales were negatively impacted due to the lack of tracking along with management's inability to help prioritize and manage the leads and their associated issues and / or concerns.

Transformation:

The company launched a change management effort to determine the challenges related to the new system. This evaluation identified the key issues were related to lack of inclusion of impacted sales teams in the process, and a lack of sales process understanding on the part of the technology implementation team.

After the evaluation, the company utilized the recommendations to develop new sales processes to speed up access to information on products and services. They also provided the sales team with new supporting technology and laptops to assist with quickly documenting and following up with leads:

How it could have been avoided

The sales team should have been engaged in the process early on to explain their current processes and their business needs. Including the impacted groups early and throughout the process would have alerted leadership to the issues with out-of-the-office activities and their limited access to load information into the system. As a result, the process and systems would have been developed to help the sales team with a full understanding of their needs and issues. This involvement would have assisted in developing a solution to improve their performance and profits.

Change Management Keys

- Engaging impacted groups early in the process to understand the concerns
- Follow-up during the process to review the address the issues and concerns
- Provide adequate and timely training to support learning the new process
- Identify process improvements to enhance the transformation effort

KEY QUESTIONS:
CHANGE MANAGEMENT

Change Management is often ignored until the project starts or until issues are identified. It is important to ask your team to review these questions to assess the focus and importance of change management:

1. Do you have a change management office assigned to the transformation?

2. Is your change management office and plan integrated across project workstreams and not just from the top of the organization? This is important to ensure that all impacted groups and levels are equally assessed and managed.

3. Has the change management office completed an assessment of the impacts of change on employees, customers, and partners?

4. Do you have a plan of communication to educate impacted groups early in the process and keep them informed and educated on the status and impacts throughout the process?

5. Will the team be completing periodic assessments throughout the process to keep management informed on changes and challenges?

6. Do you have a metrics / measurement process that you will be utilizing to review or perceive real impacts and concerns continually throughout the process? This can be

helpful to determine if individuals feel that they are being adequately supported and trained to manage the process.

7. Do you have a plan for communicating the management's understanding of impacts and your plan to mitigate issues and risks through training, support and education / information?

COMMON PITFALLS:
CHANGE MANAGEMENT

Assuming Buy in

Companies assume that employees will buy into the changes and improvements simply because it's best for the company. They don't always consider how employee see change as having negative impacts on themselves.

Assuming Communication is Change Management

Many companies assume that change management is simply providing clear communication. They believe sending out periodic emails on the status of the project and its positive benefits to the company will suffice. Although providing communication and sharing key information are critical elements of change management, they alone do not address all the issue individuals will be experience through the project. These issues can make them less prone to support the initiative and therefore impact its success.

Not understanding the impacts

It is extremely important to identify and define potential impacts of change on impacted individuals (role, income, status, workload) at the start of the process. Many companies do not fully understand the amount of change people will go through until they are in the mist of the project. At this point, it can be too late to properly prepare individuals for the inevitable change that is coming.

Not having a change champion

Transformation efforts require a change champion whose primary focus is to define and understand the changes, to coordinate with the teams, and to marshal resources to support change management efforts in the most efficient manner. These champions monitor impacted groups and their issues as they oversee change initiatives to address resource concerns.

Change at the top of the house

Embedded change management only in the program office or at the top of the organization chart will create issues with coordination across the individual teams. Change management should be incorporated into each team to ensure alignment with corporate focus and to provide feedback from the impacted groups to senior leadership in a timely manner. This coordination also helps the organization provide assistance and support throughout the process.

Lack of change management training / orientation

Project teams should be trained / oriented on change management assessments and issue identification. These teams are working directly with the impacted groups and therefore have the ability to provide firsthand information on unforeseen issues, group reactions and impressions to change management initiatives. They also provide recommendations of process, communication and training of change initiatives to improve program success. This information should be shared as part of their project status reports so they can be properly vetted, or initiate an improvement plan to address the concerns.

Lack of change management status reporting

Program and project meetings should include a designated change management reporting item. Incorporating these items into project status and program status reports will ensure leadership is aware of potential risk resulting from change management issues. This information helps to educate the organization on what impacts are expected so mitigation solutions and processes can be put in place.

Not demonstrating an understanding of change impacts

Any transformation effort will have positive and negative impacts to individuals, business functions, customers and partners. In order to enhance team buy-in, leadership should illustrate their understanding of the impacts, concerns and the challenges to the organization and impacted groups. Individuals want to know that the organization understands that impacts are coming and that they are focused on trying to address them in a way which minimizes the issues and maximizes the potential of the individuals in the organization.

PROCESS IMPROVEMENT

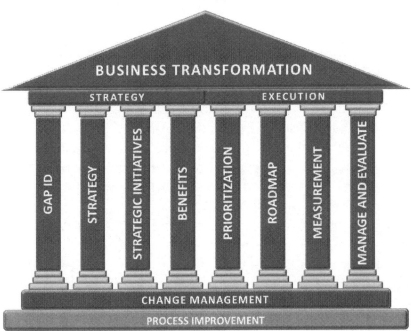

The Harden Transformation Framework ©

The Space Between Strategy and Execution | Gregg Harden

"Excellent firms don't believe in excellence - only in constant improvement and constant change"

- Tom Peters, Business Author

PROCESS IMPROVEMENT

Another important component of business transformation is process improvement. When incorporated into the transformation effort leadership can better plan and prioritize initiatives impacted by the process changes. Often companies grow quickly, but not strategically. In such cases the organizations themselves may not be efficient to accomplish their goals. This inefficiency can include organizational structure, business processes, technology and systems that support services and products delivery.

It can also include everything from product development management to the structure of the sales force or the structure of the marketing team, and even challenges with the people within the process. You need to ask whether the company has been able to bring in the right people with the right skills set to do the right jobs, at the right time, for the organization. Companies often promote or transfer people into roles based on their success in previous roles. These previous roles may not be aligned to their new responsibilities and the actual required skills set may be different and unique.

EXAMPLES OF QUESTIONS TO HELP PROCESS IMPROVEMENT

- What is the best way to motivate the sales organization?
- What's the best structure for marketing now that marketing has changed?
- Is social media for an organization best suited as a marketing element or a PR element?

- Do you have within your organization the right functional and structural components to be successful?
- Have you analyzed the business process for efficiency and effectiveness recently?
- Do you have scheduled periodic reviews of your business processes?
- Have you had a chance to look at a process by which customers are on-boarded to your organization?

Unlike many of the elements in process improvement, the skills set or the resources assigned are uniquely different than just being an expert in a function. It's a good idea to have people available who understand how to diagnose or first script out a process flow then assess the individual process elements. The next step is to determine whether there are risks or challenges within the process; Where it can be enhanced, where it can be improved. Those are all skills that often do not reside within the functional group.

EXAMPLE: PROCESS IMPROVEMENT

Company:

Fortune 500 company

Situation:

The company had determined that one of its key business units was not meeting the needs of their customers and associated sales teams. The business units' sales were declining in a growing market. As a result, they were seeking to develop a business strategy to improve business growth and profitability.

Complication:

During the strategy development project, several business functions were identified as hampering business success. The identified functional teams had inefficient business processes. The business functions leadership team was unable to adequately assess their groups performance against competitors and best practices. The improvement effort would require working across groups (sales, technology and product development / management). In the past, these areas had not been able to manage their inter-department conflicts to work together on improvement efforts.

Transformation:

While reviewing the business strategy, a process improvement effort was launched to examine current business operations and determine how they could best be utilized to support the potential new strategy.

During the process improvement project, key functional elements (product management, product development, and sales support) were assessed:

- Product development and management resources did not have the appropriate background to manage their respective areas of focus
- The groups were not structured in a manner conducive to support timely product development and active product management
- Sales teams were not receiving timely responses from their sales support resources
- Product management did not have the proper level of resource support as compared to its peers

As a result of the process improvement project, key business changes were recommended:

- The business unit strategy was reviewed and refined
- The product development and management groups were restructured to better develop and manage products and services in alignment with new business strategy
- A roadmap of new products and services were identified
- Key stakeholders (customers, sales, and external experts) were utilized to develop and prioritize the business recommendations

How it was accomplished

The project benefited from engaging an external process improvement team having experience with the business process, organizational design, process improvement methodology and access to external competition evaluation. This team was integrated with the company's project team. This integration enabled the company to leverage their capabilities to develop a process to improve efficiency across the functions. The team was able to focus on the issues and challenges without being considered biased in their evaluation. As a result, the final recommendations were accepted by all the impacted functions.

Process Improvement Keys

- Company engaged resources with process improvement experience to work with their subject matter experts
- Business strategy was utilized to align the needs of the functional support areas
- Process Improvement resources knowledge of competitor structures and organizational alignment experiences were critical to the process review

KEY QUESTIONS: PROCESS IMPROVEMENT

Process Improvement is critical to the success of your transformation program. The following questions will help you evaluate your ability to identify, track and implement improvements:

1. Do you have an internal process improvement group assigned to the transformation?

2. Is your process improvement team integrated across transformation project workstreams or only at the top of the house? This is important to ensure that all impacted groups and levels are equally assessed, if applicable?

3. Has leadership identified key focus areas for process improvement review?

4. Are process improvement opportunities reviewed throughout the transformation process to keep management informed?

5. Are the identified process improvement opportunities reviewed on a periodic basis for prioritization, approval, funding and activation?

6. Do you have a plan for communicating the impacts (financial, non-financial) of process improvement

opportunities on your transformation plan (timing and success)?

7. Does the process improvement team have a plan to communicate improvement opportunities to impacted groups?

COMMON PITFALLS:
PROCESS IMPROVEMENT

Not aligned with strategy

Improvements efforts should be aligned with the overall or functional unit strategy. These efforts should assist the business to reach its financial or operational goals. This alignment will enhance leadership engagement and support.

Wrong resources / wrong skills

Improvement efforts can require specialized skills in the areas of project management, organizational alignment, systems implementation, data modeling, etc. Companies should resist the urge to have a "smart person" look into it. This will often minimize the areas of improvement which can be assessed and decrease the impact of the improvement opportunity.

Inadequate funding

The improvement effort requires funding of the project team (resources and support) and additional funding for the recommendation implementation. If funding is an issue prior to improvement effort, the project team may not be as focused in their assessment and recommendations. If the funding is an issue after the recommendation has been developed, future improvement efforts may suffer from a "why bother" mentality.

Missing external comparisons

Most improvement efforts are internal facing, but they can greatly benefit from external information. Industry best practices are extremely useful in developing recommendations. They can provide a beacon to assess your performance and help guide your review.

Lack of cross-functional engagement

Improvement efforts often have cross-functional impacts. It is therefore necessary to work with these groups to develop process or system solutions. This needs to be coordinated to achieve the full value of the improvement initiative.

Lack of leadership support

Improvement recommendations typically suffer from the bureaucratic inertia of the institution. Leadership engagement and focus is key to breaking through this apathy for change. Without this support, the initiative will not be implemented in manner that will maximize the anticipated business improvement benefits (productivity, profitability, etc.).

TOP 20 QUESTIONS

TRANSFORMATION QUIZ

	Question: Scale 1 -5 (Poor to Excellent)	Score
1	Does your team understand the strategy behind the business transformation?	
2	Does your team understand the business gap the transformation is attempting to fill.?	
3	Does your team understand the expected benefits of the transformation (financial and non-financial)?	
4	Does your team have a clear understanding of success?	
5	Does your team have a benefits-expected statement to help guide decision making?	
6	Does your team understand how this effort fits into other strategic initiatives and the roadmap?	
7	Does your team have the experience and authority to make key decisions that may impact expected benefits?	
8	Does your team have the experience and authority to provide negative news to leadership?	
9	Does your team have the right mix of relevant business and experience and project management experience?	
10	Does your team have the ability to change scope and priorities based on changes in the business environment?	

	Question	Score
12	Have you developed a change impact assessment to determine the impact of change on employees, customers and partners?	
13	Is executive management engaged / informed on a weekly basis of the progress of the transformation?	
14	Is executive management engaged in reviewing significant issues, scope changes and risk on a weekly basis?	
15	Are you evaluating the impacts of project decisions on the expected benefits during the transformation?	
16	Are changes in benefit realization reviewed by the executive team?	
17	Do you have the ability to quickly stop this transformation if it does not meet expected benefits (not available for all efforts)?	
18	Do you have process for evaluating your project management process?	
19	Are you evaluating and assessing the project management process during the transformation?	
20	Do you have process to change the project management process during the transformation, if necessary?	
	Total	

LESSONS LEARNED

1. Provide a clear strategy for business transformation for everyone engaged to develop buy-in and commitment

2. Utilize executive leadership to manage tradeoffs in business scope, issue management, and escalation review

3. Confirm the benefits expected from the transformation to help guide decision making

4. Have a clear understanding of business needs

5. Develop or utilize relevant business documentation / process flows to confirm current state and detail needed changes for future state

6. Provide constant communication (level and specific) to ensure employees and customers understand the entire process from start to finish.

7. Ensure change management is engaged and utilized to monitor and address employee / customer satisfaction and expectations

8. Develop a roadmap of what can be done from phase 1 – phase x.

EPILOGUE

Business transformation takes place in challenging business environments and also during times of economic prosperity and expansion. Business transformation initiatives should be utilized to improve operational performance areas that have been lagging or to take advantage of new opportunities that exist. Many companies transform themselves to new markets, new products, new services, and new customer demands. Companies may also transform how they operate by implementing new technology and systems (big data, cloud computing) to support business processes. They may also use business transformation to change operating processes, operating cost structures, and organizational structures during slow economic environments.

The 8 phases of execution covered in this book are designed to guide your organization's transformation with the best chance of success in reaching your individual business goals. The importance and power of execution can never be overlooked or underestimated. Regardless of the economy, the market conditions, or the size of your company, how well you close the gap between your strategy and execution will determine your success.

APPENDIX

ABOUT THE AUTHOR

Gregg Harden is an **Experienced Business Transformation Consultant** with over 20 years of experience leading business optimization projects for Fortune 500 companies. He has significant expertise revamping business strategies and processes.

Previous Organizational Consulting Experiences:

Multiple Fortune 500 enterprises including:

- Ernst & Young Management Consulting
- Bank of America
- AT&T (Bellsouth and Cingular Wireless).
- SunTrust Banks
- Wells Fargo (Wachovia Bank)
- Home Depot
- Cox Communications
- Intercontinental Hotel Group

He also has extensive faculty experience working with both business executives and graduate level students:

AMERICAN MANAGEMENT ASSOCIATION (AMA)   2001-2007

Adjunct Faculty: Strategy, Marketing and Business Planning

- Developed American Management Association's Business Planning program for Senior Leadership training.

DEVRY'S KELLER GRADUATE SCHOOL OF MANAGEMENT   2005-2007

Adjunct Faculty: Marketing and Strategy (for MBA candidates)

Made in the USA
Columbia, SC
29 October 2020